CITRON
PRESS

PETER S. **RHODES**

Born in 1919, Peter S. Rhodes studied Architecture at the University of Liverpool from 1936 to 1939 when, at the outbreak of war, he became a gunner-surveyor. With his regiment, the 155 (Lanarkshire Yeomanry) Field Regiment, Royal Artillery, he was taken prisoner at the Fall of Singapore. After the war he changed his occupation, eventually becoming a Chartered Structural Engineer. In 1953 he moved to Northern Ireland, and in 1968 he became Chief Structural Engineer for the Northern Ireland Government. He retired in 1983. His hobbies have included amateur theatre, marionettes, geology and field sketching.

CITRON
PRESS

Fresh ideas from

NEW AUTHORS
CO-OPERATIVE

Published by Citron Press
Connors Corp. Ltd., Suite 155, Business Design Centre,
52 Upper Street, Islington Green, London N1 0QH, Great Britain
www.citronpress.co.uk

ISBN 0754400115

Printed and bound in Great Britain by Esparto Digital Ltd., Slack Lane, Derby.

A copy of this book is held at the British Library.

TO JAPAN TO LAY A GHOST

PETER S. **RHODES**

CONTENTS

PREFACE

In March 1970, I, Peter Rhodes, and my wife Dea went to Japan. For Dea it was a first visit but for me it was a second time and, in fact, an attempt to lay a ghost, but the story really begins in 1939 and with the start of the Second World War.

It has been said that for many men their war service was the greatest adventure of their lives. In the years since 1945 I have had quite a few adventures and also have been fortunate in being able to do quite a lot of travelling, in fact rather more than I did as a soldier, but still I must agree with that general assessment. Why else should I have felt the urge to make these notes? However, so-called Active Service is not a continuous experience of the exciting action as generally portrayed by the cinema – very far from it. My colleagues and I spent two years training to 'do our thing' and then spent ten weeks doing it. Moreover, only about a third of that time was spent in engaging the enemy; the remainder being taken up with getting into position, waiting, changing position, and waiting again.

Old soldiers all have tales to tell and this collection of anecdotes and reminiscences is, I suppose fairly, to be classed with them. It consists mostly of mental pictures recorded by my eyes and ears and other undefined senses over a period of about six years during the Second World War. Some of the memories are funny, some are sad, a few are rather unpleasant and many are of interest when their circumstances are compared with today's equivalent.

As I have studied the rather jumbled notes that were made, on any paper available at the time, I have been surprised at the way the memories have come flooding back. It has also been very gratifying to note that where I have been able to revisit some of the places mentioned, or even to meet again some of the people named, the memories as recorded in this essay have been proved to be almost startlingly correct.

CHAPTER ONE

I BECOME A SOLDIER

At Rock Ferry High School I had been rather a duffer, never any good at rugger or cricket. In the gymnasium, being of very light or scraggy build, I was good on the ropes and bars, but on the vaulting horse and in athletics I was hopeless. I left school in 1936 with a Northern Universities Matriculation Certificate, which listed a distinction in French and in Physics and Chemistry, and a Higher School Certificate which recorded a 'good' in Geography and in French. Then, rather misguided by the Headmaster, R. J. Griffith, because 'the boy's good at art and he likes making things', I spent three years 'up' at Liverpool, reading Architecture. For most of that period I was Guild Stage Manager in the Students' Union, but I was not very good as a student architect, being much more interested in how to construct a building, rather than in its architectural design.

In early 1939 a recruiting office for the Regular Army was set up in the University and several of my friends came out with 'tickets' for OCTU, but for me that seemed to be morally wrong. Even then I was rather a fatalist, so I did nothing and waited to see what would happen.

Some time in early July, shortly after my twentieth birthday, I was called to an office in Birkenhead to register for conscription and was interviewed by an elderly but kindly Colonel. He asked a lot of questions about my school and architectural training, my hobbies, the Boy Scouts, amateur theatre and anything else he could drag up. Then he said he was not permitted to tell me where he was sending me but thought that I should find it to my liking.

The university summer term came to an end with the usual orgy of dances, grand balls and parties - and I failed my exam! A friend of the family found me a job as a draughtsman with John Clarke and Son, Architects and Structural Engineers, in Liverpool, and I found that, dealing mostly with flour mills and their associated buildings, I quite liked the work. Then, on 3rd September 1939, war with Germany began. I remember hearing the announcement on the wireless and feeling a strange thrill. The dominant emotion was excitement, but then I was only twenty, had led a rather sheltered life, and knew no better.

My call-up paper arrived at the beginning of December 1939, and ordered that on the 15th December I should report to the 41st Survey Training Regiment, Royal Artillery, at Preston Barracks, Brighton. The paper was marked at the top: 'Potential Officer'.

After a long railway journey to Brighton I made my way to the barracks in the darkness of the early evening of a very cold December day. I found myself one of about sixty other young men, all around twenty years of age and, by and large, a very gentlemanly lot. It was then that I acquired another title and a number and learned that I must be prepared to answer to either or both.

959103 Gunner Rhodes P. S.

I soon discovered that, although I was the only one named Rhodes in that barracks, nevertheless the initials P. S. after the name were an essential addition. To be called 'Gunner' on one's first day in the army sounded rather grand. It was a pity that none of us knew what a gun looked like!

After a week of leave over Christmas, when we took home all our civilian clothes, we soon got down to the serious business of being trained as Artillery Surveyors. Our duty, it was explained, was to provide to the gunners, and sometimes to others, the accurate positions of all the regiment's guns and all the targets, so that the men at the guns could, with accuracy, hit the desired targets. This involved facility with trigonometry, and a great deal of practice in the use of theodolites and other similar optical instruments. We also had concentrated training in the use of a surveyor's chain, steel tapes, and an assortment of other gear. A piece of vital equipment was the slide rule, although we also made great use of seven-figure logarithms. None of this work was difficult but we had to be capable of doing everything at high speed and in any kind of adverse conditions, and so we practised and practised, and practised yet again.

At the end of three and a half months of concentrated training we were given inoculations and sent on a well-earned week of leave. When we returned, several parties of four men each were 'posted' as trained surveyors to artillery units going to France or already there. My name appeared on the notice board as 'attending man' or reserve for one group of four, and next day as first man on the next group. No one went sick and so the attending man was not required, and then the postings stopped and my group was 'stood down'. It was not until some seven weeks later, when the news broke about the evacuations from Dunkirk, that I realised my own good luck. Had the attending man been needed I should almost certainly have been at Dunkirk, assuming that I had survived that long. The life expectancy of surveyors was at that time thought to be very short. After a few more days of waiting, again my name appeared on Part Two Orders, together with those of Gunners J. Andrews, N. D. Polley and D. H. Robinson. We had been posted to the 155th Field Regiment, RA, in Lanark, Scotland.

Early on the morning of Monday, 15th April 1940 we left Brighton and headed for Scotland. Sewn proudly onto the left sleeves of our battledress jackets was an embroidered letter 'S' surrounded by a laurel leaf. This, in accordance with a note in our paybooks, denoted that we were 'Mustered and Appointed Trained Battery Surveyors, Group C, Class II'. Arrived at Lanark, we soon found plenty of new friends and learned that the 155th Field Regiment, RA, was a new regiment but founded on a quite old Territorial Cavalry unit called The Lanarkshire Yeomanry. Its officers appeared to be 'the gentry' from the counties of Lanark and Dumfries, while the men came from the same areas. No one saluted. They tugged the forelock! Incidentally, I gathered that the reason why both officers and men had joined the Yeomanry had been because of their love of horses.

In May 1940 we were introduced to a new arrival: Colonel Russell, RA, Instructor Gunner, a kindly man with grey hair. Colonel Russell took charge of the technical training of the whole regiment, giving guidance on how to handle field guns, how to give and to implement fire orders, and how the 'specialists' with each troop of four guns were to pass the correct 'line', as provided by the surveyors, to the guns.. Then, while the gun crews and their specialists were practising, he collected together all eight surveyors and thereafter devoted the greater part of his time to us, calling us 'my surveyors' or, later, 'my boys'. It was then that Douglas Polley and I were re-united with Jimmy Andrews and Denis Robinson, and also met four more surveyors: John Fretwell, Bobby Edel, Joe Crowther and Charlie Smith. As they figure in my memories, I should introduce them now.

Norman Douglas Polley came from Sussex and was, I think, the Westminster Bank's youngest Branch Manager. He took readily to the applied mathematics of our surveying but also was quickly put in charge of 'B' Battery Pay. As a member of the Plymouth Brethren he was in those days strictly a non-drinker.

Denis H. Robinson came from London and had been a Civil Engineering assistant. His manner of speech, in good English and a slight London accent, was always very blunt and direct. He liked to 'get going' and also hated cant and pretence. He was six feet two inches tall and for some reason had in Brighton been given the nickname: 'Tiger'. It seemed to fit him very well.

Jimmy Andrews was a well-spoken, well-educated and gently nurtured young gentleman from somewhere in the Home Counties. I cannot remember his pre-war occupation.

John Edward Fretwell came from Hoyland near Barnsley and had been a civil engineer with the Dumfriesshire County Council. He had been a Territorial in the Royal Engineers, but when he moved to Scotland the only available TA unit was The Lanarkshire Yeomanry.

Bobby Edel came from London, was well educated and quietly spoken, and had been a salesman of ladies' underwear. He was proud of his Jewish ancestry but was rather shy of talking about personal matters.

Joe Crowther came from Dewsbury, to the west of Wakefield, and Charlie Smith came from Wombwell, to the south east of Barnsley. Both were coal mine surveyors, though not in the same pit. I list them together because they always *were* together and they looked so much alike that the majority of the regiment could not tell them apart. They both had a strong Yorkshire accent, used a lot of dialect and miners' jargon, and they were always arguing or even fighting with each other.

However, if anyone was foolish enough to say a word against, or to lay a finger upon either one, then the other would fly to an immediate defence. An example of their arguing might be over an item of surveying or, when off-duty, might be about almost anything. In spite of their rough exterior they both were quite well educated and were very efficient as surveyors. Life without Joe and Charlie would have been several shades paler.

Colonel Russell always referred to us as 'The Survey Party' but in fact while we spent the major part of our days working and training together, we remained as Battery Surveyors.

In theory all ranks in the Royal Artillery should be able to drive any of our vehicles, but to achieve even an approach to this ideal needed a lot of training, simply because in those days the privately owned vehicle was a comparative rarity. My teaching came from a few of the men of 'B' Battery (I think of Bill Glencross) and under the guidance of Captain Fraser Stewart and 2nd Lt. J. P. Devine. The motor cycle was a real problem, appearing to have been designed so that it and I were always being parted. The trouble, I decided, lay in the working of the twist-grip accelerator. My problem was that, being of very light weight, when my machine hit a bump of any sort, I was bounced up and backwards so that my hand tended to open the twist-grip, thus increasing the speed of the engine. As soon as the rear wheel touched the ground again the bike would leap forward while I landed with a sickening thud on the grass or in the mud while the bike careered riderless on its way. It happened far too often for comfort or confidence. Eventually, and after a hair-raising test, my driving licence was issued by the Lanarkshire Constabulary and stated that I was tested and found competent to drive all kinds of vehicles!

Sometime during the late summer of 1940 we were introduced to our new Survey Officer, 2nd Lt. Michael Willmer, and the surveyors then became officially known as the Regimental Survey Party. It was at about this time that a third battery, named 'C' Battery, was created by means of a redistribution of both officers and men, and then, in the autumn of 1940, twenty-four guns arrived. They were not the 25-pounders that some of us would have preferred, because of their longer range, but were the older 4.5-inch gun-howitzers with an average range of 5,000 yards. In the late autumn it was announced that the guns were to be calibrated, and all the measuring and checking were to be done by the Regimental Survey Party. Six of the surveyors went onto the target area, a bleak stretch of moorland, to observe and measure the fall of shot, while Douglas and I were to be at the guns. We checked all the instruments and used a portable clinometer to check the range-drum reading against the actual inclination and the appropriate ballistic calculations. This was the first time that any of us had been near a gun when it was fired, and several of the layers, the Number 3 of the crew and the firer, were scared at first. Douglas and I compared notes at the end of the day and reckoned that between us we had fired approaching a quarter of all the 96 rounds which went over during the day.

About the end of November 1940 I was given a week's leave and was persuaded by Gunner Tom Collins, an old Yeomanry man, to borrow his suit of 'dress blues'. The suit looked very smart as I set off proudly on the train to Liverpool and home. However, I soon regretted wearing it, and for two reasons. Firstly, the material was much finer than the serge of my battledress and at the end of November the weather was very cold. Secondly, my mother, my grandmother and my girlfriend all disapproved most strongly because they did not wish to be seen with a 'chocolate box' soldier.

When I returned to Lanark I was surprised to find that the regiment had gone! They had moved to Haddington, fifty-five miles from Lanark and about fifteen east of Edinburgh. A rear guard party was packing up gear and I was to go with them to Haddington in a few days' time. Meanwhile, there was nothing to do, but I should sleep in the billet. One night I was woken by a noise and a flash of light and, looking toward the door, I saw the dim outline of a policeman. 'Yes? Hello?' I called quietly. The figure approached my bed and I recognised a Special Constable whom I knew slightly. 'Who's in charge here, Peter?' he asked. 'Sergeant Lowther,' I replied and indicated a bed. The 'Special' walked over and woke the sergeant, saying: 'I've a young woman outside who says one of your fellows has got her knickers and she's "wantin' hame".' Sergeant Lowther quickly dragged on a pair of trousers, walked to the door and switched on all the lights. Then he called: 'Wake up, all of you! Which one of you has a girl's knickers?' There was no reply so he motioned to the policeman to go and get the girl and as soon as they returned he called: 'Sit up, all of you. Sit to attention!' We all sat bolt upright in our beds, whereupon the woman, now recognised as 'Carnwath Kate', the local pro, certainly no girl and no good-looker either, conducted an identity inspection, preceded by the constable and followed by the sergeant. As they approached me the constable threw back some loose blankets on the bed next to mine and revealed a man, still fully clothed and wearing his boots. The fellow, known to me as a friendly but bucolic type, and perhaps only 'elevenpence in the shilling', sat up and rubbed his eyes. 'That's him!' shrieked Kate and then, pointing to below the bed: 'And them's my knickers!' She gathered them up and made a hasty exit, followed by a smiling constable and accompanied by a roar of laughter.

There was talk of going abroad but no date was given or suggested. I was given a week of Embarkation Leave and then I said a fond and supposedly final goodbye and returned to Haddington. However, the only move was when we all went back to Lanark.

The Survey Party, now ten in number, moved back into the old office but there was much unrest. John Fretwell applied for a commission but when, after a long delay he asked about it, he was told that his letter had been sent on to 'Command', whoever that was. Eventually he looked in the Colonel's filing cabinet and there found his letter, marked 'Hold'. Next morning he demanded to see the Colonel – and within the week he was away to OCTU (Officer Cadet Training Unit). I was sorry to lose John as a comrade, but I wished him well. He went on to take a commission in the Royal Artillery and finished the war as a Lieutenant-Colonel.

My civilian employers, John Clarke and Son in Liverpool, applied for me to be released from the Services to do 'essential' work on the flour mills and other industrial buildings which were being damaged in the air raids. I know the request reached the regiment and, like John's letter, I think it was sat on, but now that there was a chance to go abroad I did nothing about it.

Fretwell's departure left a vacancy in the survey party but, there being no time to train a new surveyor, Gunner Cyril Toye, a Londoner who had been a specialist with one of the troops, was given the job. Talk of going abroad increased, and I went on leave again on 3rd February 1941, only that time it was called 'Privilege Leave'.

Soon the rumours grew stronger. We were going abroad. Going abroad! Two simple words which conjured up all kinds of exciting thoughts. Before The Second World War few had cars and even fewer had been abroad, that being a privilege reserved for the rich. And now I was to go abroad, and at the expense of His Majesty's Government. There was a strong rumour that our destination was India. I collected notebooks, sketchbooks, pens, pencils and watercolours; all to record my 'grand tour' for my admiring family. The thought that I might not survive simply never occurred. We packed up our gear, with everything not essential during the voyage to be stowed in a kit-bag consigned to the hold. Then, early on Sunday, 15th March 1941, we were taken to Greenock and put aboard a large P&O liner, the SS Strathmore, of 23,428 tons.

The Survey Party and the members of Regimental HQ were put down on 'G' deck where there were long linoleum-covered mess tables to seat fourteen men, and above which, at night, we slept in hammocks slung from the deck beams above and at about maximum density. Some time during that night we heard the sound of engines and felt the ship moving. Next morning, another man and I went with two buckets to get the food from the galley but when we returned to the mess table no one else wanted any. They all felt seasick so the two of us had a very good breakfast, after which we returned the remainder to the galley. At about that time, however, one of those feeling sick had gone to an upper deck to get some fresh air - and returned bearing news. We were not at sea at all, but were riding at anchor in Gourock Roads. As soon as that had sunk in, the other twelve men wanted their breakfast - but it was too late!

We really did sail during the early hours of the 17th March, and for the next two or three days I had a plentiful breakfast, most of the other men being seasick once more. Going up on deck, I saw that we were in a big convoy which included at least twenty large passenger liners like the Strathmore, as well as some smaller ones and two large warships as escort. Long after the War I learned that our convoy had the code number 'WS 7'. Soon there were icicles hanging from the railings and overhanging parts of the ship. We must have been very close to Iceland and I remember thinking: 'This is a funny way to go to India!' After about four days we turned southward on a zigzag course, presumably to dodge the U-boats.

After another week things began to warm up a little and we all went up on deck as much as possible. I was invited by Wally Patten, one of the ship's stewards, to join him and his brother, together with two other soldiers: Carlisle and Horne, in a piano-accordion band. Our high spot was to play in a ship's concert called 'Tropical Follies', which ran for several nights. On the 29th March the convoy put in to Freetown for a replenishment of water, etc. We were there for about thirty-six hours and on the second day the accordion band was taken by motor launch to our sister ship, the Stratheden, where we gave an afternoon concert.

I was intrigued as we approached Sierra Leone because the profile of the hills, when seen from well out to sea, really did look like a reclining lion. As we came close to the land, I was impressed by the vibrant colours of the landscape. The whole scene shone with a brilliance of colour that I had never seen in the more gentle sunlight of even the brightest day in England. Even if sketching had been permitted, I doubt if I could have done justice to that scene.

As we sailed on southward, the weather became cooler and then, for two or three days, we were back in icy waters again before turning northward. We reached Cape Town on 16th April 1941, almost a month after leaving Scotland. After breakfast the following day we were allowed to go ashore. As we walked through the dock gates and in the direction of the town, we had hardly taken more than a few paces when cars began to stop at the kerb and the occupants were asking: 'Can we take you somewhere?' We accepted the offer with alacrity and for several thousand men that was the start of an hilarious three and a half days.

The Strathmore left Cape Town alone early in the morning of 21st April 1941, en route for Bombay, and once again a large number of men were seasick for the first few days. Late that day we were overtaken by the cruiser HMS Glasgow which escorted us for the next two days.

I didn't believe it when, hardly out of Scotland, the wiseacres and a few old hands assured us that we should be able to smell Bombay from two hundred miles out at sea. But it was true! We could!

I first noticed the odour on an eastern breeze as I stood on an upper deck after the evening meal. There was no land in sight and I was assured by a crewman that we were some two hundred miles out in the Arabian Sea, and not expected to reach Bombay until after dawn on the following day.

CHAPTER TWO

TRAINING IN INDIA AND MALAYA

On 10th May 1941 we said farewell to the Strathmore, our floating home for eight weeks, and went ashore carrying our gear. After a short walk the whole regiment climbed aboard a train, the time then being about 8.30 a.m. The first few miles were through the rather tatty outskirts of Bombay, after which the train turned east across the coastal plain. That was my first sight of a really foreign country. Cape Town had looked very much like a mixture of British towns but here was different. Firstly, there was the unremitting heat, and then the people dressed strangely. However, I did think that some of the green areas, with trees, grass and the occasional stream, resembled parts of the British Isles.

After about an hour we began to approach a line of high mountains which, I remembered, were called The Western Ghats, whose height, I later learned, was nearly 7,000 feet. Soon the train was climbing, zigzag, up the steep escarpment. The craggy scenery was awe inspiring and I wished that I could have a picture, but I had no camera and we were changing position far too quickly for even a lightning sketch. As we climbed up that huge scarp the vegetation became thinner and thinner and when eventually we emerged onto the plain of the Deccan we were in a very different world.

As far as one could see, everything was of a pale and dusty yellow-ochre colour, with just here and there the occasional domestic group of buildings or an isolated temple with perhaps one or two dusty-looking trees, generally a monotonous desert. After travelling for some three and a half hours (a distance of about one hundred miles) we stopped at Poona, where sandwiches were handed out and men in grubby white skirts, jackets and turbans came aboard with big urns of sweet tea; very sweet, almost like syrup. We then moved on for about fifty miles to a junction at Dhond, where the train turned north for another fifty miles to Ahmednagar, our destination. It would then have been about four in the afternoon.

We were taken from the railway station to the barracks and directed to our new billets in a collection of gloomy looking barrack blocks built of black basalt. By that time, about five, all were tired and hungry, and we began to ask for the whereabouts of the mess. We were told that the kitchens were not yet ready and, regretfully, would not be so until tomorrow morning. However, about twenty minutes later, we were called to file past a contractor's truck parked at the corner of the big parade ground. I was one of the first to reach the truck where we received, on an enamel plate, two rounds of bread with pats of butter, two hard boiled eggs, and a mug of very sweet tea; not exactly princely, but better than nothing. The men in front of me set off happily across the parade ground to carry the food back to their billets, but they were not happy for long. The leaders had not gone far when big birds, some form of kite, swooped down and took one or both the rounds of bread. Then a man in front of me swore loudly at the birds and held his left hand spread to protect the bread and eggs. A second later and he had lost the end of a finger! I got my plate of food back to the billet by tying a large white handkerchief over it. From that day on we all regarded those predators, soon to be know by all as 'Shite Hawks', with the greatest of respect.

We stayed in Ahmednagar for two or three weeks during the latter end of the 'summer' season. The sky was always blue and cloudless while everything else was hot and dusty. I enjoyed the general heat, although there were times when the wind was like a blast furnace. The only green colouring in miles of country was likely to be the pale emerald tints of copper salts coming from minerals in the Deccan basalts.

We did a little exploratory survey work from Ahmednagar but were not well equipped with either transport or maps. However, those trips helped us to become accustomed to the heat and to see a little of the countryside. Most of the roads were narrow and dusty and in some areas there was a lot of traffic which tended to slow us down. It consisted of pedestrians, some carrying enormous bundles on their heads, a lot of zigzagging bicycles, bullock carts, and a ubiquitous vehicle known by all troops as 'the wog bus'. These appeared to be of more or less standard design: a rather small double-decker open-topped bus with the luggage piled high on the upper deck. It was used solely by the Indians and was always so overcrowded that goods and people always bulged from it. From the sound made by those buses, we judged that the drivers used nothing but second and third gears.

The bullock cart, with its two very large wooden wheels, was drawn by two patient and long-suffering bullocks. It was a common sight moving slowly along the road, the cart full of the menfolk of the family while all the women walked behind, carrying the family luggage on their heads. Apparently, once the bullocks were set to walk along a road they would just keep on going, even if all the family were asleep in the cart. It was said that if the bullocks were surreptitiously led into a U-turn, they would continue to plod away so that the travellers would wake up back whence they had started.

When we had first landed in Bombay and had boarded the train, every man was given a packet of cigarettes and a blue-green booklet with the compliments of W.D. & H.O. Wills. The booklet was an advert for Wild Woodbine cigarettes but its twenty-two pages were advice to soldiers newly arrived in India. The booklet had been printed in 1940 but I suspect that it was written many years before that. Included was a small vocabulary of words and phrases in Hindustani, the language used between the troops and those Indians who could not, or would not, speak English. I learned as much as I could and found it essential for dealing with the dhobi (laundry man) and also when we wished to buy anything in the bazaars. However, I noticed that all the offered 'useful phrases' were in the imperative tense and that the words: 'Please' and 'Thank you' were not included.

We passed through but never stopped in sundry small villages which, mostly, were all little better than slums. We quickly became accustomed to being assailed, as by a cloud of flies, by innumerable small children, mostly very snotty and dirty looking, who held out grubby hands and cried: 'Baksheesh, Sahib!'

We were forbidden access to the town centre of Ahmednagar, being limited to the 'cantonment', meaning that area which was policed and reckoned to be safe for the troops. The cantonment area of Ahmednagar, or at least that part of it which I was able to explore, was a rather drab place with little entertainment to offer beyond a cinema, the 'Sadar' bazaar, and a rather scruffy eating house. It was in that cinema that I first noted the strange effect of coming out of a nice cool place into the almost stifling heat of the night; the exact opposite of one's experience in Britain.

Some three or four weeks after arriving in India, we stowed all our gear into an assortment of vehicles and drove the hundred miles to Kirkee, two miles north west of Poona. We found that the barracks were of a design similar to those at Ahmednagar but more pleasantly arranged and better equipped. Whereas Ahmednagar had been almost a desert, Kirkee Barracks was well supplied with trees, some of them with bright orange flowers and all offering welcome shade. They were also the 'parking place' of many cicadas whose strident whistling pervaded the whole area. However, after only a short time our ears had become accustomed to the never-ending noise and we hardly noticed it.

Just inside the main gate at Kirkee there was a stall where one could hire a bicycle by the hour, used by the whole regiment to travel the two miles or so into the cantonment area of Poona. The native city was out of bounds. I think it was on my first trip into Poona that I bought a camera as my twenty second birthday present to myself. It was a Voightlander Reflex with a 2.25-inch square negative. I had no experience of photography, other than as a schoolboy with a Kodak Brownie, and my inexpert juggling with time and aperture was not helped by the fact that the monsoon broke on the same day I bought my camera. From then on I never saw blue sky in India. However I, and many others, took a lot of photos.

On several occasions while at Kirkee, the surveyors would cycle into Poona for an evening out, the aim being to have a good meal followed by an evening of quiet drinking. For this purpose we soon found an eating house where the proprietor could let us have sole use of a back room. I had never really liked beer, much preferring whisky, but unfortunately in India it was thought, quite officially, that no one below the rank of sergeant could ever be capable of drinking whisky. Hence, a little bribery to the proprietor was needed. Then, when a round of beer was ordered, and paid for out of a kitty, I ordered and paid directly for a whisky. I'm proud of the fact that it was always I who got the party back home and safely through the guardroom. Sometimes it wasn't easy, and one particular evening stays in the memory.

All had gone well while we were indoors, but once outside and on the bicycles again, the games started, in and out of private driveways, but then Joe, followed closely by Charlie, detached from the rest and pedalled hard for home. Soon Charlie, becoming tired, turned into a side road on the left – simply because it led downhill. I found him sitting on a triangle of grass at a road junction, and with his head through the frame of his bicycle. He was loudly cursing Joe, who had ridden on although knowing that Charlie was drunk. I saw the others silhouetted against the sky as they rode past the end of the turning, and as they all seemed to be on their way home, I attended to Charlie, lifting the bike over his head and straightening the handlebars. I don't remember how I managed to get him onto his machine and moving in the right direction, but certainly it would have been impossible had I not been slightly drunk myself. Charlie appeared to be willing and able to pedal but was incapable of steering, so I rode my machine by steering with the right hand while reaching to steer Charlie with my left which, unfortunately, was not strong enough and we ended in a double heap. Reluctant to put him on the outside, eventually I changed hands and we travelled slowly up the long hill to the barracks, accompanied by the incessant croaking of countless frogs at the roadside. They even drowned out Charlie's equally incessant cursing. After a long and, for me, painful journey we all reached the barracks, where the bikes were returned and I collected the deposit money for all. Then I talked us all through the guardroom, being grateful for the fact that the duty sergeant was a friend.

In early July 1941 all the drivers and second drivers took their vehicles, a rather assorted lot, down to the outskirts of Bombay and came back with a complete set of new ones. The Survey Party went in with two Chevrolet trucks and returned with four 'Austin 8' two-seater, canvas-hooded cars and two 1,000cc BSA motor cycles, the latter being ridden by 2nd Lt. Willmer and Sergeant Jimmy Brown. The road to Bombay led down the Ghats quite near to the railway line but, although by that time I had a camera, sadly it was of no use because the monsoon weather had obliterated all the spectacular views of the mountains. Soon after reaching the coastal plain we stopped for a short break and I took one or two photos to illustrate what I thought was the 'Englishness' of some of the scenery. Perhaps that was another example of homesickness. Tiger and I had been allocated to the fourth of the Austin 8 cars, later to be named: 'Survey 4', and he drove until we had reached the plateau of the Deccan, at the top of the zigzag road up the Ghats. Then he suggested that I should take over for a while and I really enjoyed that, the only snag being a downpour of rain, for which we had to stop to put up the canvas hood. As this was a new manoeuvre it took a long time, and we both became soaked.

Not long before we left India, in early August 1941, we heard that the regiment, consisting then of three batteries: A, B and C, each with two troops of four guns, was to be split up and that two batteries, to be called B and C, were to go to Malaya. Neither I – nor any of my friends – could think of any reason why we should shed a third of the regiment but somebody higher up must have deemed it to be right. Nobody wanted to be left behind and there was a lot of moaning and groaning among all ranks when the names of those who had to move were published. The Survey Party, however, was untouched and stayed with the B and C batteries, destined for Malaya.

On 22nd August 1941, B and C Batteries of the 155(LY) Field Regiment RA sailed from Bombay in the SS Ekma, bound for Port Swettenham, now called Port Kelang, Malaya, in an unescorted convoy of five small merchant ships. For me that journey was a miserable one. I had become ill a few days earlier with a severely upset digestive system and a slight fever and, had we not been due to move, I am sure the MO would have had me in hospital. As it was, I had to travel like the others, with all our guns, all our vehicles and full kit, but I can recall nothing of the drive from Poona to Bombay, nor of going aboard the SS Ekma. I slept the first night in a hammock alongside my colleagues but then the MO did put me into 'dock' and I spent several days in a sickbay bunk-bed.

My main recollection of that journey is a smell: an all-pervading stench which was identified as various things, the most likely being sour curry. It seemed to be everywhere and in everything, including the mess food, and there is no doubt that it would have put me off my food even if I had not been so ill. After a few days the vomiting, diarrhoea and general malaise subsided and the MO prescribed 'Class 1' food for me. Being confined to my bunk, my food was brought to me, and then the difference between the food for the officers, (Class 1) and that for the other ranks became startlingly apparent. It did not smell of sour curry; I could face up to eating it; and it stayed down.

I was on those Class 1 rations for three days before being declared fit and returned to normal duties. That meant returning to the hammock and to the normal food of the other ranks, and to the realisation that the ship really was filthy. As a result, it was alive with cockroaches which came in all sizes from about an inch long to ones of three or four times as big. Far from being nocturnal, they were always on view and a regular amusement was to collect a few of the big ones and to race them up and down the long, linoleum-covered mess tables, even at meal times. Yeugh! By the time we sailed round the northern tip of Sumatra and turned south eastward into the Straits of Malacca, I was feeling quite fit again, although still very much nauseated by that ghastly ship.

Our first sight of the Malayan Peninsula, away on our port bow, was quite promising and as we drew nearer to the coast it looked very romantic, appearing to be even brighter than had been Sierra Leone. We could see mountain ranges in the distance, glowing with a purplish hue, and below them a middle ground of different shades of brilliant green. The land nearest to the coast seemed to have a dark green top over a nearly black but stalky-looking growth. Occasionally, between the land and the intense blue of the sea there were stretches of shimmering pale golden sand, but as we approached Port Swettenham and turned up what appeared to be a river, the stalky vegetation, identified as mangrove swamps, came right to the water's edge. I must admit that when seen up close it did not look at all inviting.

When, at about midday on the 1st August, we eventually came alongside the quay I was one of the first to go ashore, having been detailed to organise the local crane drivers to unload all our guns and vehicles and to have them set down in some semblance of order. It was never explained as to why that honour should have been bestowed. I was only a gunner and spoke no Malay. However, by the time the guns were ready to be off-loaded I had managed to obtain a degree of understanding and the job was done, surprisingly without any hitches.

Drivers were detailed to attend to all the transport but the remainder of the regiment were put aboard a train. This took us about twenty-five miles eastward to Kuala Lumpur and then, without stopping, we turned north for another hundred-and-thirty miles to Ipoh. The railway was, and still is, a 'metre gauge' line and appeared to be quite efficient although some of us did wonder how the surprisingly wide coaches were able to balance on such a narrow track.

The first feature of note was the lush vegetation, whether of fields near the railway line, planted trees of the rubber and palm oil estates, or the natural growth and jungle beyond. It was a remarkable and most pleasant contrast after the arid and dusty, ochre-coloured scene that generally was India as we had seen it. The second feature that stays in my memory is a demonstration of the changeableness of the weather. When we landed at Port Swettenham and during our train ride to Kuala Lumpur, the sky was bright blue, with a few large white cumulus clouds which always seemed to be in the distance. But then all changed remarkably quickly and it began to rain. Moderate at first, soon it was pelting down and then, over the rattle of the train, there came the sound of thunder and distant flashes of lightning. Suddenly there was an almighty bang as a huge spark of lightning appeared close in front of us as we watched. We all jumped and it was a wonder that no one fell out of the open windows. As the train rumbled on we could see, looking back, that a big circular patch of blackened earth was smoking in the middle of the otherwise bright green field. Later, during our stay in Malaya, we were to see many more thunderstorms, each with its spectacular display of lightning but, thankfully, we never had a strike as close as that one, which only just missed the train.

It was dark and about 7.00 p.m. when we arrived at Ipoh. There, Australians with 3-ton trucks took us about two miles out of the town to a quite extensive camp which had been constructed in a rubber plantation. In the dark we could see little of our new billets but noted that all were raised about four feet above the ground.

More Australians, already in the camp, directed us to the showers and the cookhouse and then left us to sort ourselves out. Before departing, however, they indicated an unlit lane that disappeared into the rubber trees, said that was where they lived and invited us to join them later for a drink. Quite a lot of us took up the invitation, and after a long walk we found a collection of huts similar to ours, one of which was brightly lit and throbbing with the sound of many voices. Rather timidly we walked in.

That was the instant of my first real meeting with the Australians and also the moment when I acquired another name. The full version was: 'Pommy bastard', sometimes shortened to 'pommy' but most frequently to just 'pom'. I must admit to being a little affronted by this very blunt form of address but we all soon learned that it was just a name and that we were not expected to take any offence. We also learned that the Australians, whom we soon learned to refer to as Aussies but to address individually as 'Digger' or just 'Dig', make a fetish of not giving or taking offence. Personally, I got on well with all of them and was considerably intrigued by what to me was their very fresh and practical attitude to life.

The war and its circumstances, responsible for all of us being there and so far from our homes, were hardly mentioned. All were interested in each other and wanted to hear and compare the differing philosophies. My first impression of those Aussies was that they were a boastful lot, but that was due for a complete revision later.

Next morning we were able to examine our new billets and the rubber plantation in which they were erected; the whole area being called Canning Camp. The huts were about a hundred feet long and thirty feet wide, with a floor about four feet above ground level. They were built of coconut palm timber and were roofed with a kind of thatch called atap, made from the fronds of the nipa palm. Down one long side, the front of the hut and included under the atap roof, was a balcony. The base frame at floor level was supported by many concrete posts but was separated from them by flanged metal trays rather like nine-inch square baking tins placed upside down. We were told that they were to stop the ants and termites from getting into the hut.

The rubber trees were planted on meticulously arranged grids, with the trees centred at about eighteen feet intervals. A few of the trees had been removed so as to provide minimal clearance for the individual buildings. This meant that the huts were partly overshadowed by the rubber trees, giving some concealment and also some shade from the hot sun. The plantation was still being worked while we were there and every morning, at dawn or soon after, the tappers, all men, came around to make fresh cuts in the trees. Then, just before sunset, a group of women of all ages would come to collect the latex, which they emptied from the little cups attached to the trees, pouring it into large buckets or four-gallon petrol cans. These were slung one at each end of a long and springy lath which they balanced on a shoulder.

As a Regimental Survey Party consisting of one second lieutenant and one sergeant, neither being surveyors; two lance bombardiers and six gunner surveyors, we had a lot of work. This included collecting and familiarising ourselves with as many of the Ordnance Survey maps as we could obtain and study. For the long distance work the scale was an inch to a mile; they were of good quality and of course they had a military grid. We also used 1:25,000 scale maps on the same grid for more detailed work such as locating gun positions. We practised our field work as much as we could, but soon met problems, and on several occasions I found that skills learned as a Boy Scout could be put to good use.

One of the problems was the difficulty of communication between our several small groups, usually of two men each, as we set up our theodolites on hill tops and other useful landmark positions. There were field telephones and a few wireless sets provided and worked by the Royal Corps of Signals attached to the Regiment, but we had access to none of those. Our answer was to use semaphore. I was reasonably proficient and my colleagues readily agreed to learn, and did so very quickly. We made a pair of flags for each vehicle and thus were able to pass our messages.

The Adjutant had looked with envy at our smart little Austin 8 cars, issued in India, and so, after a discussion, it was agreed that we should do a swap; one of our cars and one motorcycle for his fifteen-hundredweight truck. The car which was surrendered was Survey 4, and so it was that Tiger, the driver of the car, became the proud driver of a new 15-cwt truck with a Ford V8 engine and thereafter called 'Survey 4'. The exchange was a great boon to the surveyors because with the car and the motorcycle we had transport for ten but sleeping places for only eight, and the truck filled that deficiency.

A problem with the truck was that it was too heavy to be manhandled, particularly when it became stuck on the rather slippery ground in the rubber plantations. The answer was a length of rope, which I cut and spliced up into twelve loops, four for each of the cars, and to leave the truck always on hard ground. Then, when one of the cars became stuck, a frequent occurrence, two men were called from the next nearest vehicle, the ropes were passed round the wheels and, with a 'one - two - three', the car was lifted and carried clear of the bad ground.

The cars would take us reasonably close to the area of work but yet our surveying required a lot of walking. Sometimes this was enjoyable, after becoming accustomed to the climate, but there were times when we had to cross flooded paddy fields where quite often the water was waist deep. That was not too unpleasant, particularly on a hot day, but we were always apprehensive about poisonous water snakes, of which there were plenty to be seen. In fact, however, none of us had any trouble with the snakes, but we were constantly bothered by leeches.

When empty they were like insignificant little black worms about an inch long and about an eighth of an inch in diameter, but when full they more than doubled in length and were at least three quarters of an inch across at the widest point. Their bite was quite painless and so, if not found quickly, one was not aware of them until they were sated and dropped off the body, after which the wound would bleed copiously. There were times when, during our early days in Malaya, the first indication of having been bitten was when a colleague noticed the blood stain on one's trousers. The simplest method for removal was the application of a lit cigarette because to knock them off could enlarge the wound. It took a long time to search each other and, particularly in the north, often there would be no nearby trees or other cover for our modesty. To any stranger we must have presented a strange sight as we peered intently at each others' bare backsides.

We saw plantations of rubber trees, coconut palms, and oil palms almost as soon as we arrived in Malaya and it was not long before we met with another major industry: tin mining. One day several of us drove a few miles east from Canning Camp to a mine called Rambutan, where we were given an explanatory tour by the manager.

Someone, I suspect desk-bound, had invented an arrangement for the parking in the field, and presumably in battle conditions, of all the vehicles in a regimental headquarters. The basic idea was in the shape of a fan, with the vehicles parked at predetermined spots: the intersections of three arcs or quarter circles with various radii, and with the RHQ office truck at the centre. The RSM took it upon himself to put the plan into action and it was tried several times during exercises. However, he could never find the Survey vehicles, although the explanation was simple and practical.

Our ordained positions were at the outer LEFT-hand side of the fan, and it took the RSM a long time to discover that we were likely to be found at the RIGHT hand corner and next to the cookhouse truck. The explanation was that we had to make many long-range sorties, starting before dawn and often not returning until long after dark. Thus, in the early hours we needed to fill our flasks, etc. and then, when we returned in the evenings, tired and dirty and with aching eyes, we did not relish a quarter mile walk in the dark to get our food. However, once into battle conditions, not even the RSM could find parking areas which would permit such a ponderous arrangement - another idea conceived in the office and abandoned in the field.

During our first eight weeks in Malaya we were not under any great pressure and on most evenings we were free to go into Ipoh. Trucks carried us into the town at 7 p.m., and brought us back at 11 p.m. I went frequently but, as we were usually far away during the daytime, I saw Ipoh only once or twice in the daylight. What I did see intrigued me, it being my first meeting with the architecture of that part of the world.

Some of the name boards over the shops were in Tamil or other script that I could not read, but many had their names in Roman letters and with phonetic spelling. Some of the Chinese names caused some merriment when first seen: for instance: the name YU FAT SOON over an eating house, and SO WING KIT over a tailor's.

One of my continuing duties was to be keeper of the regiment's maps and while there was plenty of room in Survey 4 (the 15-cwt truck) it was difficult to store them tidily and safely. Quite soon, however, I was offered a large wooden packing case which, when stood on end, just fitted between the near side seat and the steel frame which supported the canvas roof. The loose lid was used to make shelves, and a front cover was made from a piece of canvas. The chest was fitted into the near side front of the truck and securely tied to the metal framework. When the canvas was drawn aside, all one could see was a large number of tidily stacked maps. Not at all apparent was that the chest had also become our drinks cupboard. None of the Survey Party were heavy drinkers but we all liked a drink when the occasion was right, and so an assortment of bottles was bought with our communal cash and stored in the bottom of the new map chest. We also were able to buy or collect an assortment of glasses which were then carried in racks made of packing case boards with notches sawn into them. The result was that we could offer a visitor a drink of almost anything he could name, and serve it in the correct glass!

When sleeping in our vehicles, the trio in Survey 4 came off much the best. The three Austin 8s were only two-seater sports cars in which it was difficult to stretch out, but I could lie full length on the padded seat down the off side of the truck. The other two, Tiger Rob and Bobby Edel, had bought themselves airbeds which they laid side by side on the truck floor.

While in India I had bought two pairs of white silk pyjamas and I argued (as an English gentleman), that if I wore pyjamas in bed, it did not matter that the bed was a seat in the back of a truck. So, whenever possible, when the time came to sleep I would put on the pyjamas and then replace my socks, boots and puttees, put on my belt, tuck my recently issued pistol into it and, with tin hat handy, would sleep reasonably well. Of course I got a lot of ribbing but eventually my friends became accustomed to the idea. It did a lot for my personal discipline, although none of the others thought to copy me. Later, for most of the time when we were in action, there was no chance at all to change clothes, but I did wear my pyjamas twice.

In early November 1941 the Regiment left Ipoh and moved about two hundred miles north to Sungai Patani in the State of Kedah. The accommodation there was almost identical with that in Ipoh: atap-roofed timber huts in the rubber trees. The town of Sungai Patani was smaller than Ipoh although the style of the buildings was much the same. We went there on several occasions for a meal but I can recall very little about it.

Our work continued much the same as before except that after the move all our sorties were northward, to Alor Star and beyond, although we did very little surveying in Perlis, the most northerly state which borders with Thailand. There appeared to be more paddy fields in Kedah than we had seen in Perak and that meant more slushing around in the flooded rice fields, all with their full complement of leeches.

It was during our early days in Sungai Patani that I invented some little gadgets to assist the general business of gunnery. One of these took the information supplied by the surveyors to the 'pivot', or Number 1 gun, and from it provided corrected figures for the other three guns in the troop. They were made of thick transparent celluloid (bought in Liverpool in January 1941, before the days of perspex) and had graph-like information scratched into them with a sharp needle.

Eventually all four Troop Commanders had a copy and my reward in each case was, if I remember correctly, a packet of twenty cigarettes. I sometimes wondered if the War Office would be interested but had no means of asking.

Off-duty time in Sungai Patani was not very interesting but a good compensation was that every now and then, with transport provided to take us about forty miles south to Butterworth. We could board a ferry boat to take us to Georgetown, the capital of the island state of Penang where I was intrigued by the Kong and Chew Piers, two projections out over the Strait and consisting of rather untidy wooden buildings, all on stilts driven into the sea bed.

CHAPTER THREE

ACTION IN MALAYA

On 7th December 1942 we heard that the Japanese, whom we had learned from our Aussie friends to call Nips, had landed at several places in the northeast and were heading south through Thailand. Our field sorties stopped and we were warned to prepare to go into action. Next day, the 8th December, our regiment with its sixteen 4.5-inch howitzers and supporting vehicles was ordered to leave Sungai Patani at dusk and to drive to Jitra, a small village about ten miles north of Alor Star. We were to travel in strict convoy with the Survey Party in the rear, on back roads and without lights because, it was said, the Nips had spotter aircraft. My fellow surveyors and I were rather apprehensive about this. Although we knew those second class and estate roads as well as anyone in the regiment, we also knew they were not very good, many being surfaced only with water-bound red laterite dust, often with pot-holes and with verges poorly defined. We arranged amongst ourselves that each car driver would touch his brake pedal frequently so that the following one would at least see the flash of the red brake lights.

Tiger Robinson was driving the 15-cwt truck: Survey 4 as usual and following Jimmy Andrews in Survey 3. Bobby Edel was sitting beside Tiger while Cyril Toye, our second driver, was in the back and peering through the little window in the canvas cover, trying to see the road ahead. I was lying on the floor of the truck, close by and parallel to the tailboard. My head was to the off side and my feet were against a large aluminium box, our water 'mule'.

After about two and a half hours of very slow progress, Tiger, who had been busy all day servicing his vehicle, called to Cyril that he was so tired he could hardly see. Accordingly, on what he thought was a straight stretch of road, Tiger came round to the back while Cyril went to the driving seat. Not realising that in fact the road bent to the right, Cyril, following Jimmy's rear light, got into first gear, into second, into third, and into the ditch! The truck landed on its off side and I, still sleeping, was suddenly awake and thought that we were under water but soon realised that in fact the cap had come off the water mule and that five gallons of water were being poured directly onto my face. Having scrambled clear and being followed quickly by Tiger, we started to shout to see if the two in front were safe. Bobby called back as he scrambled out, but there was no sign of Cyril, until we found him lying unconscious under the truck. Not being able to pull him out, Tiger and I grasped the metal frames of the canvas roof and with an immense heave we lifted the truck sufficiently for Bobby to pull him clear.

As we had been the last in the convoy, our mishap had not been noticed but, fortunately, after about ten minutes another 15-cwt truck came along and, even more fortunately, it was carrying a doctor and two medical orderlies. They were not from our regiment but were glad to help. The doctor confirmed that Cyril's right leg was badly broken and took him into his truck. He had to go forward but promised to have Cyril sent back as soon as possible. That was the last time I saw Cyril Toye but I gathered much later that he went on to fight elsewhere and survived the war.

We waited by the roadside for about an hour until one of our 'quads', the four-wheel-drive vehicles that carried the gun crews and towed the limber and gun, came along. It was a spare and had been bringing up the rear purely for rescue purposes. With the help of its winch and the reserve crew of two we soon had Survey 4 back on the road again and not much worse for its mishap, except that a lot of our gear was very wet from the five gallons of water from the mule. We got into line behind the quad, with Tiger driving again and, with two or three other similarly rescued vehicles behind us, we continued on our way north.

A mile or so beyond Alor Star we could see a blaze of light coming towards us and soon we met its source: a large convoy of trucks heading south, all with their near-side headlights blazing on full beam. All but a few had had their off-side or right-hand headlights smashed by those very irate troops who, like us, had just spent seven hours or more driving a very hazardous and extremely tiring sixty miles or more in complete darkness and scrupulously without headlights. Any of the south-bound trucks with right hand headlights still ablaze had them knocked out by members of our little convoy. A man in the back, or sometimes the driver himself leaned out and used his steel helmet.

As we passed the offending convoy it slowed down and then we realised that they were Indians. A moment later and we had further evidence of this because the convoy stopped - just like a goods train. That is to say, in the manner which to us seemed to be the normal practice with Indian Army convoys. The leader stopped by using his brakes but every other vehicle behind stopped by bumping into the one in front, with a sound reminiscent of a railway marshalling yard!

Just before dawn on 9th December 1941 we arrived at the village of Jitra, and a few miles beyond it we turned off into a rubber plantation in the area where the regiment took its first stand, generally around the very small village or kampong of Tanjong Pau. Ours was the only complete regiment of artillery present at that time and Lt.-Col. Alan Murdoch found himself also commanding a mixture of small groups of guns from several other regiments that had not yet arrived in full strength. These included anti-tank guns and a portion of an Indian mountain battery. It took some of our guns a long time to reach the positions assigned to them. and several became bogged down. I could never understand why the guns had to be sited in such difficult positions. With an average range of about 5,000 yards, the effect of a shell would be no different if fired from a much easier one.

The Colonel had found a long, atap-roofed estate hut near the northern edge of a rubber plantation and made it his HQ. Douglas Polley and I were told to set up our 'information centre' at the western end of the hut and to be prepared for action within minutes. We had a field telephone and an Artillery Board, a two foot square board with a white top, gridded with lines only but similar to a 1:25,000 scale map, which was to represent the present battle area. We also had our one-inch maps and the tabulated records from our earlier surveying. Our duty was to take calls from observation posts, gun-troop officers, and infantry officers; to plot on the board all information received and to give out the co-ordinates and other details of targets to the guns. In the days before the fighting, when we were stationed at Sungai Patani, the Survey Party had measured and walked over the present battle area. So, with the aid of our remarkably good ordnance survey maps, we were able in imagination to 'see' the whole of it as we worked at the artillery board. As a result we had a very good overall understanding of the battle in so far as it involved artillery. Seen now in very long hindsight, it was rather like being in the control room of an outside TV broadcast where the collection of monitor screens gives the producer an overall view. For me it was completely fascinating and, because we were so busy, there was no time to feel any fear.

Douglas and I stayed there for four days and nights, taking turns for the briefest of naps on the floor below the table if there was a short lull in the action. From time to time items of food and the occasional block of chocolate were brought to us by the Colonel or by Major Gerald Sanderson. A shell landed on the eastern end of the hut and demolished that part, including the colonel's table and chair, but luckily both he and Major Sanderson were out in the field at the time.

Equally fortunately, Douglas and I were not hurt by the splinters. We knew which Nip gun had fired it and we also knew that, unlike us, he did not have detailed survey information and was simply ranging. That shell was at about his maximum range and we did not expect any more. Indeed, none came. That incident was the first time I realised that all gunners, irrespective of nationality, were constrained to think and behave alike. It was in the very nature of their trade. When this thought was related to our job in hand we found that there were times when we could predict the fall of enemy shot with some usefulness to our own gunners and to the infantry officers who called us. It was a truly fascinating period, albeit in a horrible way.

Eventually, for reasons well documented in the histories but not fully understood by us at the time, the Jitra front collapsed and just after dark on the 13th December we were ordered to pack up our gear and withdraw to a nearby kampong (village). There our friends the cooks gave us some hot stew and a pint mug of tea which had been liberally laced with rum. Douglas and I ate the stew and drank the tea, grateful for such comfort after our four days on bits and pieces, then we both lay back on the earth floor under the hut and slept, dead to the world. Little more than an hour later Lt. Willmer woke us and told us we were all to move out and south to a new front somewhere in Kedah. I found that the brief sleep had been so deep that the previous five days and nights without any real rest were forgotten and I was once again quite fresh, although I should very much have liked a shower and a shave.

We found our respective vehicles and as Tiger drove Survey 4 slowly through the rubber trees in the darkness of the early evening, heading for the main road to Alor Star, we saw in the sky to the north of us three signal flares. Red over red over red, which meant only one thing: every man for himself! Suddenly I felt slightly sick, and I don't think it had anything to do with the large quantity of rum recently imbibed. Apprehension was increased by the sight of remarkably young Indian troops running through the rubber trees, throwing away their equipment, some kicking off their boots, and many shouting: 'Run, Sahib! Run!' All of us were affected by this, and I can honestly say that it was the first time I really understood the soldiers' expression: 'Shit scared'. Every time the truck stopped, usually because the way was blocked by other vehicles all trying to reach the main road, I had to dash off into the trees for a 'rear'.

When eventually we got onto the road we found that it was crowded with vehicles, head to tail and all heading south at a crawl. We wondered why the pace was so slow until about a quarter of a mile further on we found the obstruction. A troop of four 25-pounder guns had decided to stop, one behind the other, to lighten their limbers and were firing at nearly full range in a northerly direction. I have no idea what that miniature barrage did to the enemy but obviously it invigorated the gunners who were cheering and yelling as they reloaded. It helped us too, in a strange way, but it also meant that we had to drive apparently straight into the gunfire. The 25-pounder always made a big flash, much more than did the 4.5 howitzer. When seen from the front and at night those four guns were most impressive and I shall always remember the scene.

My all too frequent need for the toilet continued until the next day when we re-grouped and prepared for battle once more. This meant more surveying and while we looked for good observation and triangulation points the trio in Survey

4 found ourselves on top of Kedah Peak (Gunong Jerai), a rather isolated eminence in the middle of Kedah State and several miles north of Sungai Patani.

There we met an elderly Indian gentleman who insisted on giving us a cup of fresh-brewed tea. Then he insisted on showing us around his garden and pointing out some of the many different trees and shrubs. I can remember only a few of them now but I do recall sampling the Golden Banana, or pisang maas, which is quite small but has beautifully rich-flavoured, golden-coloured flesh. He also showed us durian and jack fruit, explaining the difference and showing us how to eat them. The jack fruit was quite nice but I did not like the durian, even though assured that it is considered to be a great delicacy and that monkeys will travel miles for one. Finally, he asked us if we had ever seen coffee growing, and indicated a lot of bushes at the side of the path. When we each picked and bit one of the seeds there was a semblance of coffee flavour but not what we had expected. Of course, the seeds were barely ripe and they would have to be roasted to produce the real flavour. After all our tasting, our new friend again insisted that we must have another cup of his excellent tea before we went on our way.

I felt sorry for that old gentleman, alone on top of the Peak with his beloved garden. He knew that the Japanese were coming and that he might be killed, yet he was quite calm and seemed to have no fear and no anger. I wished that we could take him with us but, when we offered him a lift, he declined with great courtesy and dignity, saying that he must stay with his garden.

We returned to our old camp in Sungai Patani for a brief rest which, lasted for three nights. When on the 8th December we had left our camp to go to Jitra we had been told to leave our kitbags behind, to be collected later, and now we hoped to recover them. Unfortunately, during our absence others had been in the camp and had moved our gear. Some of it had been ransacked but we of the Survey Party had been able to take with us all of our more cherished possessions, in tin boxes I had made from empty petrol cans, and carried mostly in Survey 4. My own kit bag contained only spare clothing but I was very glad to be able to retrieve it as I was urgently in need of a change. Since leaving Sungai Patani there had been absolutely no chance to do any laundering; in fact it had been difficult enough to find the opportunity to wash oneself.

The camp was deserted when, bit by bit, the 155 arrived. There was no electricity and so our first night was rather difficult. However, we were glad to drop onto any string bed, or charpoy, that we could find. Then we discovered, rather to our disgust, that all the huts had been invaded by rats. They were huge and we could see them scuttling across the floor and along the timber wall plates under the eaves of the atap roof. Next morning a foraging party found a number of traps in the almost deserted town, and these were set with whatever bait was available. The result was amazing! The creatures were completely naive regarding traps and we had little sleep that night because of the banging of the traps, which were reset as quickly as possible until we ran out of bait. Then someone set a few without any bait and to our surprise we went on catching rats; so much so that a burial party was needed when morning came - and the next night was peaceful.

After the brief rest at Sungai Patani we moved north and once more into action between Bedong and Gurun and it was at this time that we made a discovery which materially altered the performance of our regiment. We had noticed in many places, such as at the corners of rubber plantations and paddy fields, little posts of stone or concrete, about four inches square and eighteen inches tall. I suggested that as these were obviously survey pickets there must somewhere be maps on which their positions would be marked. Most of the country around us was already deserted and so we began a systematic search of all buildings which looked like estate offices, and quite soon our efforts were rewarded. We found a drawer full of very detailed estate maps to a scale of ten inches to a mile and, after a brief study, located the hut and the nearest mark that looked as though it might be a picket. We went out to look for it and, sure enough, we found a little concrete post. So far, so good, and we took all the maps and stowed them on the floor of Survey 4 with a groundsheet over them for protection.

The immediate advantage was that if by survey we could 'fix' (or determine the co-ordinates of) just two of those pickets on any one sheet, then we could give very accurate military co-ordinates for any desired position, gun or target, that came within the boundaries of that sheet. A further exercise was to find a formula whereby, without that preliminary fieldwork, we could relate any estate map to the military grid. Tiger and I sat up all one night and at the cost of a full bottle of gin and rather a lot of scrap paper, by morning we had two warm and sticky slide rules - and the desired formula. Much later in the campaign we met a man from the Ordnance Survey who, when told about our formula, said we need not have bothered because he knew it very well. Unfortunately, our meeting with him was rather late; we had been using it for weeks!

Our gunners were experts at handling their pieces and when their specialists were given the accurate information which we were now able to produce very quickly, the result was an almost frightening accuracy of fire which earned, with at least one regiment of Gurkhas the nickname of 'One Round Johnnie'. With that degree of accuracy our 4.5-inch howitzers, firing 46lb shells, could take out a small road bridge with a single round. I developed a strong affection for those little posts.*

It was about this time, while still in Perak, that I noticed a peculiar behavioural phenomenon which I called 'The Wagon Lines Complex'. When the men were at the guns and busy, they felt that they knew their enemy and were doing something about it. I would not pretend that anyone was really happy but at least there was no sign of the debilitating fear such as I had experienced after the collapse of the Jitra front. Away from the guns, however, things were often rather different. If a man were to suffer a minor injury, then he was likely to be sent back to the wagon lines to have the wound dressed. Being usually a long way behind the guns, one would expect there to be a generally relaxed air in the wagon lines but, on the one or two occasions when my duties took me there, I found the exact opposite to be the case. One could still hear the guns and at night their flashes lit up the northern sky. The nearest Nip must have been miles away but yet, so far as I could see, many of the men in the wagon lines were imagining them to be lurking behind every tree. The result was that all too many had diarrhoea!

The only cure appeared to be to get the man back to his gun as quickly as possible. Of course, the gun crews knew very little about the overall state of the battle and none of us knew then what the longer term future would bring. The

In '*The Bitter End*' by Holmes and Kemp, published in 1982 by Anthony Bird Publications Ltd, there is a comment on page 113 about Major General Murray-Lyon of 11th Indian Division and the retreat from Gurun, 15th December 1941: 'The Japanese, mauled by the accurate defensive fire put down by Murray-Lyon's artillery, did not follow up closely, and by the morning of the 16th the remnants of 11th Division were behind the (Muda) River line.'

important thing at that time was that they thought they knew, and were actively fighting the enemy. There had been times when, visiting the guns in the course of my duties, I had heard the crews shouting and cheering with every round they banged off. Unfortunately, several men whose duties kept them in the wagon lines were not able to 'enjoy' that kind of cure and perforce had to stay in semi-ignorance and consequent anxiety, if not real fear.

At frequent intervals the surveyors would have to update information and 'fix' new points. Some of these were the positions of our own guns, which for safety reasons did not stay long in the same place, but we were also interested in possible targets such as bridges, road junctions, corners of woods, etc. I recall one such expedition somewhere in mid-Perak when Tiger and I carried all our gear to the top of a small hill, leaving Bobby to guard the truck. To mark our position for other surveyors we erected a beacon of red and yellow bunting, under which. Tiger set up the theodolite. He had just started to call out the angles for me to 'book' when we both realised an unfortunate fact. Not only could our fellow surveyors see the beacon but so could many other people, and they were treating it as a target. Bullets were going both ways through the bunting; British coming from the south and Japanese from the north. Tiger had done a left and a right traverse at great speed before demanding, fair dos, that I should take the remaining two traverses. We changed places and it was then that we both were mindful of and grateful for all the drill that had been imposed upon us. As soon as the last figure was in the notebook, Tiger toppled the beacon while I grabbed the theo, still on its tripod, and we removed ourselves as quickly as possible from the firing line.

The Survey Party had one range finder, with a one-metre base. It was carried in a large and well-padded tube-like case, but even so was a very inconvenient extra burden. Also, only two or three of us could use it with any acceptable degree of accuracy. I was the only one who wore spectacles and it was virtually impossible for me to make a reliable reading. However, others who did not wear glasses found difficulty in adjusting the eyes to line up the two images. In fact, although we rehearsed the use of the rangefinder both in India and Malaya, during the ten weeks of fighting it never left the truck. We had better and far more reliable methods for getting good results.

The next incident recalled is when we retired once more, this time back to Canning Camp, Ipoh. Muddy and dirty, bitten by mosquitos and leeches, unshaven and scarcely able to see through a theodolite for lack of sleep, I dumped my equally dirty gear under the first unoccupied charpoy I could find, flopped down on it and slept soundly for six hours. When I awoke I was told that Captain Stewart wanted to see me and in fact had been looking for me some five hours earlier. Apparently he had come in person but had been unable to wake me. Hastily I washed and shaved and smartened myself up as much as possible, even finding some blacking to put a ghost of a shine on my paddy-sodden boots. Then, a little after dawn, I reported to the Captain.

'Ah. Rhodes!'

'Sir?'

'Are you quite rested?' There was a touch of sarcasm in his voice and I knew that he, like I, was remembering the morning, oh, so very long ago in Lanark when he had found Polley and me, quite legitimately, asleep in bed at about ten in the morning. But Frazer Stewart was a kindly man and, after a brief pause, with a smile he continued: 'Rhodes, can you operate a cinema?' I didn't know how to answer that one but he quickly explained that he wanted me to go with one or two of my colleagues into Ipoh, to break into the cinema there and see if we could put on a show for the troops. I knew that Gunner Vic Ledwidge had been a projectionist before the war and so he was found and told to join the little party.

The side door of the cinema was carefully forced open and Ledwidge and I set about a quick inspection. The first thing was to see how many films, if any, were in the building. I think there were only two, of three and four reels each, so I immediately suggested to Sergeant Brown that he take Survey 4 to the railway station to see if there were any there. In due course he returned to say that my hunch had been correct and that he had the whole of 'Tobacco Road' and two shorts.

Meanwhile, Ledwidge and I set about getting things to work. All the electricity was switched off. We found that the switches and fuses were scattered round the building in a most illogical way, but we soon had some general lighting. Then we found the controls for the stage lighting, but we could not find the source of direct current for the projector arcs. Eventually, in a small and remote room Ledwidge found two large AC motors connected directly to two equal sized DC dynamos. We found the switches for the air conditioning but all they did was to control the fans which pulled in the outside air. After another hour of searching I discovered that the cooling depended on large quantities of water falling the full height of the building over vertical screens - and there was no water in the building!

By that time we had been in the cinema for about seven hours and the first night's audience would soon be arriving. Lt. Willmer, now acting as house manager, was asking if we should soon be ready so I abandoned the problem of the cooling system and joined Ledwidge in the projector room. While he threaded up the first two reels and arranged the others in running order, I found a 'magic lantern' and, using some of our Indian ink and one of my smallest paint brushes, I made a 'Welcome' slide which also bore an apology for lack of cool air.

I never saw any of those films and, except for 'Tobacco Road', I cannot remember their titles. Ledwidge and I took turns to attend to the projectors while the other re-wound the reels because we hoped to repeat the show. We had two very successful evenings in spite of the lack of cool air, but it was on the third night that the fun began. The troops arrived on time, parking their vehicles close by, as had those on the previous nights, and the show ran smoothly. Then, about half way through, the projection room phone rang and I answered it.

'Projection Room.'

'This is the house manager.' I recognised Michael Willmer's voice.

'Rhodes here, sir.'

'Can you do anything to call out the East Surreys?' I found a blank slide and wrote the message:

'SORRY TO STOP THE SHOW
ALL EAST SURREYS
PLEASE FALL IN OUTSIDE
GOOD LUCK BOYS'

Ledwidge stopped the film and on went the slide. This was the signal for a fairly orderly withdrawal of the East Surreys, accompanied by a lot of stamping, cheering and shouting. After a few minutes the telephone rang again: 'House manager here. Please carry on with the show.' About one and a half reels later, the phone rang again. 'Projection room'. 'House manager here. Call out the Leicesters'. The words EAST SURREYS were carefully wiped off the slide and LEICESTERS was substituted, and then the earlier business was repeated, accompanied by more shouts of encouragement. Yet another similar summons left only the 155 in the house and I thought we might see the end of the show but, alas, no. The phone bell rang again. 'Projector room'. 'Rhodes, call out the 155. Look sharp!' 'Yes, sir. Be with you in a few minutes.' This time the slide was wiped clean and re-written:

FALL IN THE 155
THAT'S US LADS
SEE YOU OUTSIDE

Ledwidge stopped the projector and switched off the arc as I put on the slide. Then both of us picked up our steel helmets and fell in outside as ordered. I never knew if anything else was switched off. It was all working when I left - except for the air conditioning!

The main road from Ipoh in the State of Perak runs close to the foot of the jungle-covered hills that are the western limit of the mountainous backbone of the Malaya Peninsula. To the west of the road is a coastal strip about thirty-five miles wide, much of it very marshy. About twenty miles south of Ipoh a jungle-covered mountain block, about ten miles long and five miles wide, and called 'Gunong Bujang Melaka', has been separated from the main massif by the action of two small rivers. The Sungai Siput flows to the north, while the Sungai Chendriang flows out at the southern end. A narrow road follows the valley bottom all the way round the isolated block.

The main body of the 11th Indian Division were positioned to defend the broad coastal strip from Kampar, about half way along the outside of the mountain, and across to the coast. The 155 and an anti-tank battery, supporting a regiment of Gurkhas, were detailed to hold the Siput-Chendriang defile. About five miles north of Kampar our vehicles turned off the main road and eastward through the little village of Siput, after which the road swung to the south. We set up our gun positions about half a mile south of the bend, with the Gurkhas a little in front of us. The Colonel found a small track leading up into the jungle on the east side of the road and about a quarter of a mile behind the guns. He sited his HQ truck well up the hill and Lt. Willmer with the Survey Party followed him.

There were no estates in that neighbourhood and therefore no estate maps or handy little pickets. Our only maps were the one-inch ordnance survey ones and so we had a lot of surveying to be done quickly. Survey 4 was detailed to fix some of the northerly points in the Sungai Siput valley and so, early next morning, we drove past our gun positions and made to go through the Gurkhas' lines. No infantryman likes to have people walking out through his lines and so we were challenged by our friends, with the familiar grin but great firmness. As our ability to communicate was limited to a grin and 'Hello, Johnnie.' we perforce had to dismount and walk through their trenches to explain our presence to their officer. He knew what we had to do and waved us on our way with his best wishes, but even so his Nepalese friends still looked apprehensive as we drove off in the general direction of the enemy.

Almost at the westward bend of the river we came to a single Malay house, in front of which was a large flat grassy area, obviously an old flood plain of the river. In the middle of this was a large tree which bore a goodly crop of large round green fruit, probably pomelo, a type of grapefruit. We had stopped to admire the tree when an elderly Malayan woman came from the house and smilingly gestured towards the tree, inviting us to help ourselves. Our joint knowledge of the Malay language was extremely limited but I indicated the three of us: Edel, Robinson and self, and said: 'Tiga, teri makassi' (Three, thank you). The woman seemed surprised and indicated that as there were hundreds of fruit on the tree we should take more. She stood and watched, making encouraging sounds, as we climbed the tree and collected twenty or more. We put them in the truck and Tiger and Bobby found some chocolate which they proffered in exchange. This was gratefully accepted, and we tried to tell our friend that she was in a very dangerous place and should move. I'm sure that she understood but she made it very plain that she had no intention of moving. As with our Indian friend on Kedah Peak, there was nothing more we could do short of forcibly putting her in the truck. Sadly, we left her and drove away.

Just north of the house and its little clearing, the river and the road had to turn left and westward because straight ahead were huge cliffs of bare limestone with jungle growth on top of them. The cliffs were of interest to us because they constituted a barrier with crest-clearance problems if the gunners wanted to hit targets on their far side and on the coastal plain to the north. We did our work, fixing the co-ordinates of several salient points and also checking the height of the cliffs, after which we returned to our base. As we passed the house we received a wave from the lady, but we never knew what happened to her or to the big tree of which she was so proud. We set aside nine of the big fruits, one each for our Party, and we left the remainder with the Gurkhas, receiving in return some even more expansive grins than usual.

There had been occasional firing during the afternoon of the 24th December but then the Colonel called for absolute silence until 06.00 hours on Christmas Day. Meanwhile, we gathered that OP (Observation Post) officers had reported quite a lot of enemy movement just north of those limestone hills and also at the entrance to the Sungai Siput valley. Our slide rules and those of the specialists at the guns were busy that evening, producing all the information needed to hit a large number of identified targets. When, at 6 a.m., the dawn came, the Nips received their Christmas present. Hundreds of rounds were fired by all our fourteen howitzers (two having been abandoned in their boggy sites at Jitra), so much so that the crews had to pour river water down the barrels to cool them. The gunfire was reduced after midday and then the Colonel ordered that from 18.00 hours until 06.00 hours on Boxing Day not a single round was to be fired. It would then be Johnnie's turn.

When darkness came, we, waiting back at our guns, expected to hear rifle and machine gun fire but there was silence, broken only by the sound of the river and the animal and bird noises that always come from the jungle. I suppose that there were also insect noises but we had become so accustomed to the never ending sound of crickets and other insects that we never noticed them. We waited and waited, ears straining eagerly, but it was some three hours later, at about 9 p.m. that we first heard the screams and yells that continued well into the night.

Next morning at first light several surveyors had to go forward once more to fix some newly required targets and OP (Observation Post) positions and this entailed another walk through the infantry lines. Far from being apprehensive, as on the previous occasion, the Gurkhas were clearly delighted to see us and eagerly beckoned us down into their shallow trenches. All of them had small cloth bags rather like those in which, as a child, I had taken my slippers to school. They insisted that we should look into all their bags and this we did. They were full of human ears!

Later that morning all the surveyors were back at our vehicles parked up the little lane. We were busy completing the calculations and plotting the information gathered on our dawn sortie, when Colonel Murdoch came down from his office truck, saying: 'I need a Don R [dispatch rider] and both of mine are away to the guns and the Gurkhas. You surveyors ride motor bikes, don't you.' In theory we all did but in practice we had just one, a huge 1,000cc BSA, normally ridden by Sergeant Jimmy Brown or, sometimes, by Lt. Willmer. However, neither of them wanted to be a Don R and they had the rank to defend their contention that they should not. There was a quick discussion and, like it or not, Gunner Rhodes was elected. The Colonel then explained to me that our Christmas Present to the Nips had used up a lot of ammunition and he wanted an order for a new supply to be delivered to the dumps which were at Bidor, some twenty miles to the south.

As explained earlier, I never was very good on a motor bike and such a big machine scared me stiff. Besides, at only nine stones I did not have the weight or the strength of leg to start it. Sergeant Bill Robertson, the MT Sergeant, kicked it over for me and held it while I scrambled onto the thing. Then, in first gear, I bumped down the steep and slippery track and out onto the road. I rode carefully along, over the watershed and down the Chendriang valley, passing through the deserted village of the same name. After about six miles the road bent to the right to join the main road south from Kampar, and at the junction, on the right, there was a small patch of grass, in the middle of which four Gurkhas were sitting. They were obviously eating their lunch, and as I passed they hailed me: 'Hi, Johnnie!' and they beckoned me to stop and join them. I should have liked to do so but I had an important message and if the engine should stop, I might not be able to start it again, so I simply waved back and rode on.

At the 'ammo' dump I delivered the Colonel's message, got a receipt and with scant ceremony turned and rode back the way I had come. At the road junction I turned right for Chendriang and there on the grass were the four Gurkhas, apparently just finishing their lunch. They hailed me again and this time I stopped, parking the bike with its engine ticking over. I walked across to the four who were sitting there in a little circle with, in their midst, a large white enamel plate. And on the plate was a Nip's head, cap and all!

That Siput-Chendriang defile was very secure, and in his *The History of the British Battalion in the Malayan Campaign 1941–1942*, Chye Kooi Loong records that the Japanese lost a lot of men, being mauled by the Gurkhas and the gunfire of the 155. It was the general opinion that if we had been supplied with ammunition and food we could be there yet. All my friends remember it as being quite a place.

I don't remember much about Slim River, which is a pity because it was a significant point and a very sad place for the 155(LY) where we lost a lot of men, including Lt. Col. Alan Murdoch.

The Survey Party always shared out the work as fairly as possible. And so, as Tiger Robinson and I had been continuously busy on the 5th and 6th of January 1942, we were off duty on the 7th and resting in a Malayan hut beside a plantation, on the west side of the road, about a mile south of Slim River bridge. Those out on fieldwork were Joe and Charlie in Survey 2, and Lt Willmer on the motor bike with Bobby Edel riding pillion.

The only event clearly remembered is that I was woken from sleeping on the floor of the hut by the sound of a plane passing just overhead. I scrambled quickly to look out of the window and just caught a fleeting glimpse as it disappeared to the south. At that moment Sergeant Jimmy Brown had emerged from some nearby trees and walked across a small clearing towards the hut. As he did so he opened up a large map, which must have been clearly seen by the Nip fliers. The sound of the engine died away, but the plane returned only seconds later and a small bomb was dropped into the clearing. It made a lot of noise, and some splinters shot through the atap walls of the hut but fortunately no one was hurt.

We heard sounds of gunfire to the north, and a short time later a message came by a Don R, ordering us to move to a rendezvous some ten miles to the south. It was not until evening, when our colleagues should have rejoined us, that we realised that they had met trouble. Lance Bombadier (L.Bdr.) Edel had been killed but I never heard how or where, and Lt. Willmer was captured and taken to Pudu Gaol in Kuala Lumpur. Gunners Crowther and Smith were cut off from their car and eventually were captured. They rejoined us later as prisoners.

After the major withdrawal from the Jitra front, and the succession of smaller retreats from our positions in Kedah, there was a growing sense of frustration and some noticeable anxiety amongst the Survey Party and the gun crews, whom we visited every time they changed position. These feelings were not helped when the news filtered through that the warships Prince of Wales and Repulse had been sunk. Nor were we given any confidence in 'Higher Command' when we received orders and words of supposed encouragement which, generally, were assessed as: 'Bloody silly'! One of these messages, passed on and eventually read to the troops by their immediate officers, assured us that the enemy was little more than an ill-equipped rabble who were known to do a lot of shouting. Our response, we were assured, was to 'fix bayonets and charge', when we should find that 'the enemy would melt away'. My surveyor colleagues and I had to do quite a lot of our work in what, once upon a time, was called 'no man's land'. In the early days our only weapons were Lee-Enfield rifles, but with so much survey equipment to carry, often shoulder high as we sloshed through flooded paddy fields, these were usually left in our vehicles. So far as I can remember, none of us had a bayonet but even if we had, none of us would have known how to use it.

Another 'silly order' from on high at that time was the announcement that Japanese motor cyclists wearing crash helmets had been seen. Therefore, any motor cyclist wearing a crash helmet was to be shot on sight. Normally, the Don Rs of our regiment wore the standard British steel helmet, but when I asked the Claydon twins, the Colonel's own two Don Rs, if they had ever received such an order, they replied emphatically that they had not. Only an hour or so after receiving the order to shoot on sight, we saw a motor cyclist in a crash helmet coming south down the road a little to the left of where four of us were removing leeches after a trudge across some paddy. None of us had a rifle and so there was no shot, which was just as well because, looking through my binoculars, I could clearly see that the rider was British, though not from our regiment.

It was interesting to note, however, that while most of us were apprehensive and had serious doubts as to whether 'Command' knew what it was doing, I personally did not experience another bout of fear like that at Jitra and, so far as I could observe, neither did anyone else. The word 'Command' is used because while occasionally the name of some General or Staff Officer might be mentioned, it meant very little to the mass of Other Ranks and I suspect that within our regiment the Colonel was the only one who knew much about the officers concerned. In fact, of course, so long as all within the regiment knew and understood the immediate chain of command, and could function efficiently in accordance with our training, there was no need to know any more. Or was there? Seen now after more than fifty years, the ultimate result was inevitable, but certainly at the time we might have felt a little better if the troops could have had more confidence in 'the top', irrespective of whether it was really justified or not. I suspect that on many occasions Fred Karno turned in his grave!

A side comment could be made about a much over-used expression of that period: 'You are not paid to think.' Just for fun, some of the surveyors began to 'collect' incidents where it was used, prompted by the notion that thinking was an essential part of our work, and of the gunners as a whole. We soon ticked off all the ranks up to Sergeant Major, and then heard our own Second Lieutenant receive the admonition. My personal moment of triumph came when I heard Lt.-Col. Murdoch told that he was not paid to think. The two officers were standing by the Regimental HQ truck and Survey 4 was parked close by. As it was pouring with rain at the time, both officers were wearing capes and thus were unrecognisable to a stranger.

Another 'silly order' handed down to us was that we should not fire at Nip aircraft. I never understood why. The Nip planes flew up and down the main roads, looking for stray trucks, when they would dive down and drop a bomb. On one occasion the crew of Survey 4, and the truck, were in the rubber trees close by the side of the road when we saw this happen. As the plane dived down I could see that there were two men aboard, one behind the other in open cockpits, and at the critical moment the rear man lifted a black-painted bomb which looked like an ostrich egg with fins - and simply dropped it over the side. That particular one missed its target but there was plenty of evidence in the form of burned out vehicles all along the road to prove that the method could be very effective.

Soon after the mishap at Slim River, Tiger and I were ordered to take Survey 4 south to a reference point in Negri Sembilan State. There we were to collect another 15-cwt truck and take both another fifty miles to just beyond Tampir, where the Regiment would meet us later. Just north of Kuala Lumpur and on a straight stretch of road, we were stopped by a Company Sergeant Major we did not know. He warned us of a Nip plane which was hunting that stretch of road - and he planned to shoot it down! Apparently he had already collected a few passing 'volunteers' and he invited us to join his party. His idea was that we should drive off the road and well into the rubber trees and then run back to the road with as many small arms as we had or could carry. The 'bait' was an unserviceable 15-cwt truck on the west side of the road, facing north.

The CSM said that the plane had already seen the truck but had flown away to the south. He expected it to return at any moment and to attack from that direction. Lying across the broad grass verge between the road and the plantations were several tree trunks, and when some of these had been piled quickly together on the east side of the road, three or four men, including the CSM with a bren gun, lay down behind them. The remainder, Tiger and self among them, stood behind trees on the east side. Sure enough, after only a few minutes the Nip plane returned from the south, overflew the 'bait', circled round and came in for a second time and a bombing run.

That was when about a dozen men fired at it - and we brought it down! Some of us had Lee-Enfields; I and one or two others had recently issued tommy guns. Every fifth round in my circular magazine was a 'tracer' and so I could see that several of my shots actually hit the plane. Not, however, that I would claim the killing shot. In all probability the pilot crashed out of sheer surprise. There was a big bang as the plane landed, probably caused by the already-primed bomb, and then it burst into flames. We pushed the bait truck off the road but as the plane was on the western verge and burning fiercely, we just collected our vehicles and left the scene. Everyone had a sense of great satisfaction but it was a pity that, because of silly orders, we dare not boast about it.

Eventually the Regiment, depleted and bruised, was assembled in Johore Bahru and then bumped its way across the Causeway to Singapore Island. The immediate approaches to it had been bombed several times so that the roadway, alt.hough still passable, was pitted with craters, and there was mud everywhere. The five remaining members of the Regimental Survey Party waited by the left-hand side of the road just outside Johore Bahru and watched the rest of the Regiment go by, and then we took our customary places at the rear. Thus Sgt. Jimmy Brown, Lance Bombardier Robinson and Gunner Rhodes were the last members of the 155(LY) Field Regiment, RA, to leave the mainland and cross to Singapore. As the various trucks and the gun quads, each towing its limber and gun, rumbled and bounced past us we called to many of our friends, but in spite of the apparent cheerfulness, I had a feeling of sadness and of impending doom. Darkness was just upon us when eventually Tiger drove Survey 4 onto the road down to the Causeway, and then I had a personal mishap. At one of the bigger bumps, on the Causeway itself, my small pack was bounced out of the truck and Tiger, with other vehicles behind him, could not stop. That meant that I lost a mess tin and a Rolls Razor, both being sadly missed in the days to come.

One of the first orders received from Lt.-Col. Gold, who took over when Col. Murdoch was killed, was to take Survey 4 to Fort Canning in Singapore town and get a supply of maps of the island. Three of us: Tiger, Jimmy Brown and I went on that expedition, sitting three abreast on the front seat as had become our normal way. All went well until we were approaching Fort Canning when an MP stopped us, demanded to see our paybooks, wanted to know where we were going, and then refused to let us pass with three sitting abreast. Apparently the rule was not more than two because, we gathered, it made the place look untidy. Sergeant Brown protested, drawing attention to the fact that there was a war going on only about ten miles away and we needed to keep a look out for Nip planes, but to no avail. The MP would not give way so I got down, recited my number, rank and name and demanded that he should make a note of them, but suddenly he did not want to do so. I insisted, and as soon as he had finished writing I climbed back into my seat and, without another word, Tiger drove on, leaving the MP scratching his head. Another MP tried to stop us at the gate but that time we just swore loudly in chorus and drove on.

We stopped and I went to find the map store while Jimmy and Tiger looked for a place to park the truck. I soon found the map room and was greeted by a smiling Chinese man standing behind a long counter. I produced a list of what was wanted and in silence the Chinese pulled out the maps from racks below the counter. When we had reached the end of my list and there was a big pile of maps, he pulled them towards him, tidied the heap, and counted them. Then he asked for payment, and I cannot remember the exact sum, but it was hundreds of dollars. 'Oh, no,' I said, 'I'm not paying for them. They are for my regiment and we need them urgently. There's a war only a few miles away'. The Chinese shook his head and started to draw the pile towards him, so I pulled out my as yet never fired .38 revolver and pointed it at him. He still hung on to the maps, but at that moment Tiger came through the door to give a hand with carrying the maps back to the truck. Seeing me with my pistol in my hand, he immediately pulled out his own revolver, pointed it at the Chinese and said: 'Hands up!', explaining later that he could not think of anything else to say at the time. The Chinese did not put up his hands; instead he pushed the big pile of maps in my direction and disappeared down behind the counter. I stuck my pistol back in my belt, with some difficulty picked up the big pile of maps and walked rather unsteadily backwards to the door, covered by Tiger. At the truck which was quite near and guarded by Jimmy, we dumped the maps in the back and then, sitting three abreast, drove as quickly as possible out of Fort Canning and back to RHQ in the north. No one actually tried to stop us but we were followed by a succession of shouts. 'What a way to run a war!'

While still 'up country' we had heard an assortment of stories, some purporting to be fact and others frankly jocular, but all intended to show that those in Singapore, notably those in command, did not seem to be aware that there was a war almost on their 'highly-polished' doorstep. All that we had seen on that expedition seemed to confirm these tales.

Our first gun positions on Singapore Island were near the north coast in the Serangoon district to the east of Nee Soon, and Tiger and I were called out to fix the position of a troop a few hundred yards to the east of the Jalan Kayu Road. I quote that name now, having taken it from a tourist map, but at the time we knew no such names, only recognising the roads from our maps. We drove east along the Yio Chu Kang road and stopped at the junction with the Jalan Kayu road from where, looking north, we could see a considerable length of the Jalan Kayu road slightly below us. The guns we were to visit were somewhere to the right and to be reached, we supposed, from a side track some 1500 yards north of us. In that area there were many clumps of small trees with grassy areas between, We could not see the guns or their 'quads' but assumed that they were concealed among these trees.

Tiger turned and drove northward along the road but we had not gone very far when a small shell burst on the side of the road some two hundred yards ahead of us. A few seconds later there was a similar burst some distance beyond our proposed turn-off. We rapidly agreed that the Nip was ranging and equally quickly agreed upon the likely point where his third round would fall. Tiger accelerated and at some fifty or sixty miles per hour we shot down the road and past the anticipated spot. A couple of seconds later there was a bang behind us and we both grinned, remarking only that the Nip seemed to have his line quite well. The fourth round landed near the road at about one hundred yards north of our turn-off just before we reached it and then, when we were about fifty yards along the side track, the fifth hit the junction. We stopped for a moment and I climbed on the bonnet to look through my binoculars at the junction. I was happy to see that the crater was to one side and quite small, so we and our gunner comrades would still be able to get out by that route. Tiger turned Survey 4 off the road and drove a short distance eastward through mixed trees.

Soon we came to our given map reference and found Sergeant Ginger Brown and his crew on the Number One, or 'Pivot' Gun, with the other three guns of the troop further east. We set up a 'bearing picket' a little to the west of the Pivot Gun, but in a position where it could be seen clearly from all four guns. We fixed its position and identified a good RO or Reference Object, from which bearings could be taken. We were all packed up and ready to depart when we were hailed by our friend Ginger.

He was obviously very proud of the new gun position he had chosen, and he wanted us to admire it. We were shown, and genuinely admired, the excellent field of view northwards across the Johore Strait, the good firm ground into which the trail (the rear end) of the gun was well embedded, and above all Ginger boasted of the good camouflage. The gun was by the side of a big 'Flame of the Forest' tree and beneath a sturdy overhanging branch, over which had been thrown a large camouflage net. Yes, it was a good position and Tiger and I suitably expressed our admiration.

We were just about to depart when there was a shout from somewhere to our right. Ginger stopped us for the second time, saying that Fire Orders were coming in and we should stay to see a really good crew at work. Then, turning to his men, he urged them to: 'Do it properly, lads, just to show these snooty English surveyors!' (Yes, we were good friends!)

Immediately the whole crew did everything strictly in 'drill order', kneeling 'to attention' as the ammo was passed from limber to gun, and with Ginger standing proudly to attention at the trail. The fire orders were shouted through a megaphone by the Troop Lieutenant (I cannot remember whom), and were duly received and implemented. Then Ginger, still standing to attention, raised his right fist and shouted: 'Number One Gun Ready, Sarr!' There was a brief pause, then came the shouted order to fire, repeated immediately by Ginger: 'Number One Gun, Fire!'

There was the expected bang and suddenly the strictly disciplined crew started to dance around like madmen as they tossed away their steel helmets and tore off their shirts. Tiger and I, standing a few yards away, were both amazed and amused, but it took only a moment to understand such strange behaviour. It was indeed an excellent gun position but what Ginger and his crew had not noticed was the long line of red ants that had climbed up the tree trunk and out over the big branch and the net above the gun. When it was fired, all the ants fell off onto the heads and shoulders of the crew below. Being Ginger's friends, Tiger and I departed immediately. It would have been very unkind to linger.

A sad postscript is a story I heard a long time later. Ginger moved to another position in the same general area, but in the hurry and stress of the moment, and with enemy rounds coming in, they forgot to look up the barrel. Their first round from that position hit a nearby tree and killed Ginger and all his crew.

One day during our first week on Singapore Island, Tiger and I were somewhere in the Nee Soon area, fixing a gun position, though I cannot remember which one. I was about fifty yards away from Tiger and the truck when, suddenly, there was a very loud bang which I immediately thought was a 25-pounder gun in the trees just to the south of me. Not knowing of any other artillery units in that area, full of curiosity I walked over to the trees and bushes but could see no sign of any gun. I was just about to return to the truck when I heard above me and to the south the noise of what I took to be a small aircraft. A better description now would be a noise similar to that made by Hitler's 'flying bombs'. I scanned the sky in the direction of the sound and then saw its source. What looked like a small bullet was moving across the hazy blue sky and making a large chevron-shaped wave pattern, just like those I had seen on high-speed photographs of a bullet in flight. I then realised that the very loud bang had not come from a 25-pounder in the next field, but from one of the big coastal guns on the south coast at Changi, some twelve miles away to the east south east.

The 'small bullet' was one of the big shells at somewhere near the crest of its trajectory, perhaps some five thousand feet up. Fascinated by the sight of the big shell in flight, I watched until it dropped out of sight, somewhere in the direction of the Causeway. I was halfway back to the truck when there came a very loud and rewarding 'crump' as it landed. Tiger and I moved on about our surveying business and we heard several more loud bangs, but we never saw another shell in flight. I had often heard the sound of artillery shells coming in, producing a characteristic sound of rushing, whistling, and a rapid 'chi chi chi' made by the driving band, but the noise made by that big one was quite different and I wondered why.

About a week after crossing to the island, Lt.-Col. Gold set up his HQ in some houses and bungalows around a group of tennis courts in a residential area on the west side of Singapore town and I, with several other men from RHQ, dropped my kit on the floor of a deserted bungalow on the east side of the square. By that time our guns had withdrawn into the town area and had no further need of surveyors. Therefore, for those last few days, the five of us: Sgt. Brown, L.Bdr. Robinson, and Gunners Andrews, Polley and Rhodes, just stayed in the square around the tennis courts. My recollection is not of idleness but rather of a very noisy and uncomfortable time.

On several occasions while we were still on the Malaya peninsula we had seen groups of twenty-seven bombers flying south in a strictly triangular formation, on their way to bomb Singapore. Then, when we were working in the north of the island, we saw similar groups flying over. However, I never saw any returning after dropping their bombs. On these later occasions, when the city was only about ten or twelve miles away, we could hear the rumble as the bombs landed. I think it was two days after we moved into 'tennis court square' that a group of planes came over, apparently directly above us, and as I watched with growing apprehension I could see a burst of tracer from the leading plane. That supported the story that only the leader had a bomb-sight and he gave the order to drop by firing his guns.

At that moment Douglas Polley and I were standing on the roadway outside the bungalow where we had billeted ourselves and, with no more than seconds to spare, we looked for somewhere to shelter. The only place we could see was a storm drain cut into the grass verge between the kerb of the road and the fence of the front gardens. It was lined with two-foot square concrete paving flags set at 45 degrees, but at the bottom was a half-round concrete channel with a diameter of about one foot. Douglas and I dived into the ditch and lay full length but unfortunately that half-round channel was just too narrow to take any part of one's body, so lying there on one's back was most uncomfortable. I had only just pulled my steel helmet over my face when with a swoosh and a roar followed by ear-shattering bangs, down came the bombs all around us and, for what seemed like an eternity, they kept on coming.

I was quite sure that was the end of me but, rather to my surprise, I felt quite calm and quietly resigned to my fate. There was a pause in the cascade of noise and, with ears singing, I cautiously lifted my 'tin hat' to see what was happening, but I hastily replaced it. Looking up, the sky was dark with moving objects, in fact big clods of soil, all hurtling upwards. Another second or two and all that mud came roaring down again, landing with great thuds. To our great surprise, none landed on us although all around was covered with the stuff. When it was all over and the planes had flown away we climbed out of our uncomfortable trench and looked around. There appeared to be a number of large craters and some of the houses had been damaged but, so far as I could see, nobody was hurt.

Two or three days later, I think on the 14th February, we had another raid which was almost a duplicate of the first. I was alone on that occasion and once again could find nowhere better than the storm drain. Several men had gone into a domestic shelter in the front garden of a bungalow on the west side of the square and, such is the unkindness of fate, although only a few of the bombs landed in the square, one of them scored a direct hit on that shelter.

The three or four bodies were dug out by their grieving friends and buried, with a short ceremony, in a common grave at the side of one of the tennis courts.

On or about the third day in the square, we came under attack from trench mortar shells that tended to rattle around among the buildings and their outhouses before exploding. We could not tell from which direction they were coming and, having seen that they would go through the tiled roofs of the buildings, there was really no place where one felt safe. Those mortar attacks lasted several days We also had several attacks from Nip aircraft which came low over the rooftops and used machine guns on any moving objects. There was a Bofors anti-aircraft gun close by and to the north of us and it fired away noisily at every plane that came into view. So did we, with rifles, tommy guns, or anything we had. I doubt if we did much damage but action did a lot to help our flagging spirits and the general feeling of hopeless frustration. Then one day the Bofors gun hit a low-flying plane and brought it down. After a moment of general silence, we could hear the cheering coming from seemingly miles around.

At night the noise of battle continued, coming mostly from the north. Sleeping on the hard floor without any bedding was difficult enough, but for the last few nights I found that sleep was almost impossible. There seemed to be someone with a big drum, being beaten every two or three seconds to produce a peculiar 'do-ingg' sound, while someone else had a corncrake rattle, and the two kept at it all night long. In addition the occasional mortar shell landed among the houses but they were not so frequent as in the daytime.

CHAPTER FOUR

PRISONER OF WAR IN CHANGI

It was late in the evening of Sunday,15th February 1942 that I and the other gunners attached to the 155's RHQ, gathered around the tennis courts, heard an unofficial report that the British forces had capitulated, but nobody was surprised. In fact, we had been expecting it. Slowly, as the evening passed, we became aware of a strange silence, an absence of the noise which for the past week had been our daytime 'music while you work' and our night time lullaby. The beating of the big drum and the chatter of machine guns somewhere to the north of us had stopped. No mortar shells rattled down amongst the houses, and there were no Nip planes to fire at. Just an all-pervading and rather eerie quiet. But then the silence was shattered by a series of very loud noises, best described as a mixture of a loud bang, a 'do-ingg' and a mournful whine. Some of us had heard that sound before and we felt very sad, knowing that it was the death cry of a gun destroying itself. An uncapped round is pushed point first into the muzzle of the gun or howitzer and then, using a very long cord or rope, a normally loaded round is fired. I never saw this operation but was told that most of the gun crews were overcome with emotion.

After that, at about 8.30 p.m., the quietness returned but the RSM went round the square and warned everyone to stand-to with all the small arms we had and to form a guard ring around the whole area. As there were only about forty men, of all ranks, in the square at that time it was clearly impossible to make an external ring and so it was quickly agreed that we should guard the four roadway entrances and the gaps between the houses. The RSM started to direct men to the various locations but soon found himself outvoted. The men gathered naturally into small groups of friends and, seeing this, the RSM murmured something about having fought together as friends, we might as well end the war the same way. I found myself with the other four surveyors at the north eastern entrance road and facing north, the direction from which we expected any attack to come. We spent the whole of that night until dawn lying in the roadway with our heads in the gutter and with our assorted weapons pointed vaguely northward over the pavement. Seen in retrospect, it was a pointless and futile attempt at bravado but at the time it seemed to be the right thing to do. There was an occasional scrap of conversation, interesting because all that I heard related to things far away, mostly to pre-war events at home. I dozed a little, as I am sure so did the others.

Soon after dawn official confirmation of the capitulation came and we retired back to our vehicles in the square. Some breakfast was produced and eaten, but I cannot remember what we had. Then came the order to stack all our weapons in the roadway, ready to be handed over to the Nips. The total did not amount to much and it took five surveyors, working covertly, only a short time to break or to bend all the firing pins and thus make the weapons useless. All, that is, except one; a Boys anti-tank rifle. In the end it was done by a sergeant and two men wedging the butt end over a partly open house door and swinging from the end of the long barrel to bend it.

Our next covert action was to take some lump sugar from the kitchen truck and to insert a handful into the petrol tank of every vehicle. The Motor Transport boys assured us that they would not go very far after such treatment. Then I turned my attention to our survey equipment. There was no specific order to hand over any of it but clearly it could be of value even if not of immediate use to the Nips. Equally clearly, whatever our future was to be, we could not keep it. We gave a rather expensive looking pantograph which we had 'collected' somewhere in the north to a Chinese man who lived in one of the houses in the square. Then I removed the larger lenses from all the optical instruments I could find, and pocketed the lot, while other instruments were damaged and so made useless. There was talk about escaping but the only conceivable way out was by small boat, and none of us had even the remotest idea where to find one. In fact, we had never seen the harbour, or even the southern shore of Singapore Island. In the end, none of my immediate comrades made the attempt.

We heard that Lt.-Col. Gold, with BSM Charlie Roadnight, Sgt. Lindup and one or two others had been ordered to attempt an escape and to take the Regimental records with them. Neither my friends nor I envied them, but we hoped that they would be successful. Colonel Gold could never have been called a popular man but he was well thought of as a brave and competent soldier, as was BSM Roadnight. He was also a hard man, but for all that he was well liked by all who worked with him. Those two were, I think, the only professional soldiers in that little party; the others being wartime men like the rest of us. On that day, the 16th February, nobody knew what our future would be and the best we could hope for was to become prisoners of war, but none of us had any idea of how long that might last. My own muddled thoughts were that it would be for quite a long time. At least a month, I thought, and maybe even longer! How little did we know! Another fleeting thought was a doubt as to whether we should be able to have a decent breakfast. At the time, early afternoon, I was beginning to feel hungry and there had been no opportunity to eat since a hurried breakfast. Visions of bacon and eggs tended to intrude.

Our next instruction, again via the RSM, was to pack up all the personal kit that we could carry on our backs and prepare to march to Changi, and this produced another unspoken reaction. March? To Changi? Why, that's at least fourteen miles, and maybe further from here! And gunners don't march, do they! Surely there must be some transport? No, of course not. The Nips didn't bring any, and we've just put sugar in ours. But...but...could the gear all be carried in one truck while we march?

So ran our rambling thoughts but the answer came at about 11 o'clock next morning, the 17th February, when we picked up all we could carry, fell in as a rather ragged looking three ranks, and began to march. As we made our way out of the suburbs and towards the north side of the town, we met other small groups, and although I saw no more men from the 155, soon we were part of a long column, all heading for Changi, at the eastern corner of the island. The wind had been blowing steadily from the west, as evidenced by a big plume of black smoke which for days had poured from several burning oil tanks in the Naval Dockyard, away to the north. Thus, our location at the tennis courts was to windward of the centre of town. However, as we moved to the east we noticed an unpleasant smell that rapidly grew to a horrible and all-pervading stink. It was the stench of death, of burned and rotting flesh, and it stayed with me all the way to Changi. No! That's not right! I can smell it still.

As the marching column passed through parts of the city we could see the havoc and mess caused by the shelling and bombing. In one street where there were tram tracks, the overhead power wires were hanging down but the current was still flowing and there was a continuous cascade of sparks. Most of the buildings were damaged, some very badly, In two places along our route there were big craters in the roadway, and the column had to edge its way around them, There were numerous dead bodies, mostly from the native population and including many women, lying in the streets. Several of the female corpses I saw had their skirts pulled up over their heads or were naked from the waist and had sticks and such like pushed up their vaginas. (In one instance I saw a British Army Officer's baton so used.) Also, completely revolted, I saw a bitch terrier similarly treated with a large twig.

Out on the Changi road there were more signs of the recent battles, and also of later 'enemy action'. We passed numerous corpses lying on the side of the road or hanging over the hedge or fencing. Mostly they were Chinese or Malayan but I saw two Indian soldiers, their bodies hanging over a wire fence but with their heads separately on the ground below them. Oddly enough, there was no blood and it was obvious that the already dead bodies had provided practice for a sword-swinging son of Nippon.

At one place along the road, I suppose because it was more or less straight and slightly undulating, I had a long view both ahead and to the rear. As far as I could see in both directions there were troops. I heard later that more than 65,000 men had made the long walk but, later still, I heard that the number was nearer to 85,000. However, at that time such figures were of no interest at all. The only things I knew or cared about were that I was very hot and thirsty, my feet ached, the straps of my pack had rubbed sores on both shoulders and I just wanted to sit or, better still, to lie down. There were no official stops and the trudging and hobbling column was urged on its weary and sweaty way by the occasional Nip soldier; incidentally, the first that I had seen at close range. Some stared impassively and just waved us on with their rifles, but one or two appeared to take delight in a more forceful urging, with their weapons used as goads or clubs. On two occasions someone near me tried to start some singing but it soon fizzled out. The habit of jauntily whistling 'Colonel Bogey', with its implied rude imprecation in the first two bars, did not begin in my hearing until some months later. On that first and very tiring day we just stumbled along in sullen silence. However, because of the length of the column and the large number of men, there was a tendency for it to move somewhat like a caterpillar. Parts became bunched up and thus slowed down, sometimes coming to a halt which might last a minute or two, while other parts opened out and were thus able to travel at a greater speed. One bunching up period around me lasted for several minutes and we were able to sit down on the road, but that short-lived and solitary occasion was the only rest I had.

Many men, thus tried, realised that they had started out with more than they could reasonably carry and so, from about the halfway point on, the roadside became littered with cast off objects. Steel helmets were the first to go, although I hung on to mine, possibly because I had no other hat. I had not seen my cloth side hat since we were somewhere near Slim River. My steel helmet eventually joined a few others as a hanging flower basket under the eaves of a hut. We came to Changi Gaol, on the right side of the road and easily recognisable because of its shape and isolation, but my part of the column did not slow down. The gates were closed and there were two Sikh soldiers on guard. We later learned that the Sikhs were not at all our friends, but of that more later.

Eventually, at about 5 p.m., I and my friends arrived at Changi, finding ourselves with perhaps two or three hundred others, just sitting on a grassy slope below Roberts Barracks. My journey had lasted about six hours and I remember calculating that the average speed must have been about two and a half miles per hour. I flopped down on the grassy slope and just gasped for about fifteen minutes but then I realised that I was exceedingly thirsty and my water bottle was empty. I dragged myself to my feet to look around for a possible water supply, and saw that about forty yards away near the top of the slope was a queue of men holding water bottles and other small containers. I joined them and then saw that they were receiving slow but scrupulously fair attention from a grey haired warrant officer who was presiding over a tap, presumably put there for the use of the barracks ground staff. It was running very slowly but after a wait of about twenty minutes I was able to refill my bottle. There were men sitting all over the grassy slopes below the barracks buildings but I could only recognise a few from the 155. As the daylight ended, and with no indication as to where we should go, my friends and I were too exhausted, both physically and mentally, to go searching in the dark. We simply spent the night where we sat.

Next morning word went round that there was some food available and we joined a mixed queue to receive three hard and plain biscuits and a one-inch cube of 'Bully' beef. There was nothing else. Soon after that, the RSM collected the scattered members of the 155 and led us to some beds on the first floor of one of the barrack blocks. They were packed in, almost side by side, and there were men from other units at the far end of the floor. Still feeling great uncertainty, I did not unpack anything immediately, but lay down fully dressed on the charpoy-type bed and slept dreamlessly for about three hours, making up for the past two nights. I think most of the men around me did the same. About noon I found the showers and enjoyed a good clean-up; the first I had had for three days. We received two 'meals' a day, each of two dry biscuits and a very small piece of bully, and we stayed there for four days.

Then, on Saturday, 21st February 1942, somehow all the men of the 155 were gathered together and we marched back down the road and into Changi Gaol. It was intended for 650 prisoners but when we arrived all the cells appeared to be filled, mostly with three men or more in a space intended for one. I never knew who they were. The men of the 155 had to make do as best we could in the workshops and corridors. I had a space of about six feet by two feet on the concrete floor of the tin plate workshop, and slept there for eleven nights. Throughout that period our rations, now issued by our own cooks, continued as before, with two biscuits and a minute piece of bully twice a day. At the beginning, and for the first few days, I had been ravenously hungry, but gradually I became accustomed to that minimal diet and the hunger pains became less acute. Later, on the first day in the gaol, we were ordered to hand in all watches and cameras, so I bent the escape wheel on my watch while my camera, a Voightlander Reflex, 'lost' its lens. For the first three days we were confined to the gaol. There was a library there but, by the time I had found it, all the English books had gone, so I took two French novels, titles long forgotten, and read them both.

Early on Tuesday, 24th February, I was pleased to be sent on a small outside working party. However, the euphoria didn't last long because I soon discovered that we had to clear the beaches. Looking back on my time as a prisoner of war, this was not the most arduous nor the most dangerous job I had to do, but it was certainly the most nauseating and revolting. Our little party, consisting of a sergeant and three men, were given four spades and a very dirty stretcher and we had to 'tidy up' the beach nearest to the gaol for a length of about six hundred yards. The job did not seem to be too bad as we walked down to the shore, enjoying a little freedom from the close conditions in the gaol, but as soon as we saw the beach we were horrified. There seemed to be corpses everywhere, some washed up on the sand, others bobbing about in the shallows. There was a line of Chinese women and children, all roped together and all shot in the back of the head or in the back. I cannot remember the number but there would have been more than a dozen, half of them children. I later heard of more similarly roped and shot groups on other parts of the shore. To carry them they had to be cut apart, and I had a small pocket-knife, but the flesh was so bloated that I could only cut the ropes between the bodies. All of that line wore Chinese clothes, the women being in the typical baggy 'pyjamas', but most of the separate bodies were naked. All appeared to be from the local native population. Two, I remember vividly, were almost completely buried in the sand and were only found because one of the men stepped on what he thought was a smooth stone, only to discover that it was a protruding buttock, which farted at him. He gulped loudly and went quickly away to retch. All the bodies were bloated and stinking and we had to drag them ashore or dig them out and then, on the stretcher, carry them a short distance inland and bury them in one big hole. That grisly chore took two days, after which I spent the whole day in the gaol, reading the French novels as avidly as I could.

On Friday, 27th February, I was again summoned to do an outside job and immediately prepared to protest. However, 2nd Lt. Ronaldson, an architect, quickly assured me that this was different, and an attempt to lessen our overcrowding. I was to go out by myself and look around between the gaol and the shore and to find, inspect, measure and sketch any buildings which might be usable as billets. He gave me some paper, a pencil, a piece of stiff cardboard and a battered linen tape with the first foot missing. I enjoyed that little job and found several small but useful buildings which, given a tidying and a sweep out, would certainly be better than the claustrophobic and grossly overcrowded conditions in the gaol.

On Wednesday, 4th March, a number of men of the 155, including myself, moved out to the huts I had located. Others had been to tidy them. It was good to get out of the gaol but there was no change in the rations and there were mosquitos and creepy-crawlies in abundance. However, our new discomforts were short lived because, only two days later, on the 6th March, the whole regiment was put together in an area called Birdwood Camp, about a mile west of Changi village. It is now a part of the airport. We were housed in atap huts more or less identical with those we had in Ipoh and in Sungai Patani, and we each had a charpoy-type of bed; absolute bliss after the hard concrete floor. We soon discovered that all the troops of the 11th Indian Division had been gathered together into Birdwood Camp and that, under Japanese instructions, strong barbed wire fences had been erected round it and also the Australian Lines, Hospital Area, and Southern Area. Each area had a single gateway onto the road which ran roughly east and west through the middle of the prison camp complex. We could move freely within our own area, but individual prisoners were forbidden to go out of it. Special permission was needed for small parties to do so, and they had to be accompanied by a special banner bearing mysterious oriental writing. I later discovered that one of the prominent symbols thereon was the Japanese phonetic FU, short for *furio*, or prisoner of war.

We also discovered that there were very few Japanese soldiers anywhere in Changi, but that the gates and fences were manned by renegade Sikhs who had joined Bose's Liberation Army, and by Koreans who, to this day, are regarded by the Japanese as inferior citizens. Both of these groups took great delight in insisting that all prisoners, and particularly our officers, should salute them.

Failure to do so with alacrity and smartness brought an immediate punishment, usually administered with one or other end of a rifle. We soon learned to take the easy way and many officers, when going near those sadistic guards, would endeavour to conceal their rank. This needed positive action in the early days but later, as our very limited supply of clothing and razor blades ran out, all the prisoners looked alike, equally scraggy, scruffy and minimally dressed.

The British, and even more so the Australians, appeared to have an innate ability to produce some sense of order out of chaos and so very soon a regular pattern of life emerged. Birdwood Camp had been built to house Indian troops and there were latrines, showers, water taps and kitchen areas.

Within an hour or so of going into that camp our cookhouse was working and meal times were published. There appeared to be a modest supply of rice, although how it got there I never knew. There was very little other food but, even so, it was a great improvement on our previous meagre rations The big problem was that our worthy cooks had no experience whatsoever of cooking rice. The result was a soggy and greyish, sticky mass which was served to us in the form of a rectangular dollop, cut from the unappetising mass in the kitchen pot. With this we received a cupful of 'stew' consisting of a small amount of bully beef in a large volume of water.

This watery diet did strange things to our digestive systems. Everyone found it necessary to go to the urinal at about half-hourly intervals, day and night; and throughout the twenty-four hours there was always a steady. stream of men walking to and from the urinals. On the other hand, with so little solid and fibrous food, the need for a 'rear' was surprisingly infrequent. Not having been for a week, I reported to the MO, Captain Seed, who smiled understandingly and said: 'When it has got to a fortnight, come back and see me.' In fact I and many others settled down to a 'once every ten days' routine, and this gave the opportunity for some jocular comments, such as: 'I knew a fellow who went once a week - and he never missed!'

Another oddity arising out of the unusual diet was 'Changi Belly', when all of us developed distended abdomens, so nearly hemispherical as to be quite comical. This also was a little worrying at first but our doctors assured us that it would disappear after a while, as indeed it did.

I stayed in Birdwood Camp for exactly ten weeks but I can remember very few incidents of any great significance during that time. Although we were strictly confined within our Area, for the most part life was smooth and discipline was good, though more in a civil rather than military sense. Most of the officers and NCOs in my orbit adjusted well and quickly to the new requirements for authority, but it must be said that one or two behaved rather unwisely. To survive in those conditions, both individually and as a group, everyone had to be something of an 'Admirable Crichton'. A few young subalterns, perhaps feeling that they were somewhat inadequate as leaders in those conditions, would back up their quite legitimate commands by adding: 'If you do not do so, you will be shot!' This was clearly an invocation of our Japanese captors because the prisoners had no means for carrying out such a punishment. I never heard of anyone being shot by the Japanese for such domestic misdemeanours.

I had one personal brush with authority when, about two weeks after we had moved into Birdwood, the RSM ordered me out on parade a full hour before the published time, when the ration fatigue party was to leave our camp area. Having twice before had a similar order, and on each occasion having had to stand at ease but hatless in the hot sun for about an hour, I refused to go out. I sent a message to say that I should be happy to pull the ration trailer at the appointed time.

The result was a minor explosion. I was paraded before the Orderly Officer, found guilty of disobeying an order, and was sentenced to seven days 'detention'. As all of us were already detained, this meant that I was confined to my billet hut, though of course permitted to make the frequent trips to the 'lats'. Another gunner was nominated as my guard and he also had to bring my food to me. Happily, he could play cards and the week passed pleasantly. Soon after the hearing the Orderly Officer, Captain George Hinton, came to see me in private and apologised for the sentence, explaining that while he understood and sympathised with my action, it was considered necessary to maintain a show of discipline. Next day I received with my food many messages of approval and encouragement and was glad to note that no other fatigue parties were called out so unnecessarily early.

When my detention was over, the RSM ordered me to take charge of the latrines and I had no doubt that it was a rather small-minded attempt to extend my 'punishment'. However, it was not known that my earlier training had included sanitation and hygiene. I took the job as a challenge and spent nearly eight weeks improving the general conditions of the toilet area. There was no piped sewerage system and no means of providing one, but the underlying silty clays inter-bedded with layers of sand were very absorbent. Thus, boreholes of about 16 inches in diameter and about 20 feet deep appeared to be the answer. There were already several such holes when we moved into the camp but their tops were poorly protected, they had obviously been in use for too long and also were badly sited. A bucket auger was found, with a team of six men to work it, and I marked out positions for new holes in lines along the contours of the sloping site.

Paving flags were brought in from areas of little used pathway, and four of these were set over each hole so as to leave an open slit, 2 feet long down the slope and 6 inches wide. This, I had discovered by experiment, made balancing in the squatting position much easier and also simplified the washing down process. A record was kept and each hole was left open for two weeks, after which it was closed for the next two weeks with a concrete slab over it. A check of the soil brought up during the boring had indicated that the important sand layers were more or less horizontal, so every day I inspected the lower levels of the slope to make sure that there was no unwanted leakage. Happily, during the time I was there none appeared.

The 'bogs' was the place where news items, real or imaginary, were retailed and discussed. Because of this, any piece of new information, or any rumour, became known as a 'borehole'. There were some amusing anecdotes about the place, some being unfit for publication. One story relates to a gunner, I think from the 5th Field Regiment, RA, who had some tattoos on the lower part of his back or, perhaps one should say, on the upper part of his bottom. There would always be a laugh from the squatters in the upper rows when before them over a borehole in a lower row there appeared two large eyes and above them the letters: I C U! Another anecdote, heard much later, told of a small, bespectacled and mild-mannered man, a chartered accountant from Singapore. His name was Lancelot Cowin but he was known to his friends as Tommy. One day a kitten fell down one of the boreholes and would certainly have died but Tommy tied a rope round his ankles and had some friends lower him head first down the narrow and unsavoury hole to fish out the kitten.

In the early days the open boreholes became the source of thousands of flies, but I arranged for some box-shaped nets which were suspended inside a light wooden framework. These were then placed over a hole which had been closed for the previous two days with a piece of ply-wood. Then, when the ply-wood was removed, a swarm of flies would rise up towards the light and into the net. The bottom corners of the net were then untied from the frame and bunched together before the top corners were released. The whole net bag was then quickly immersed in a big pot of boiling water. Of course, there were still numbers of flies around the other holes, but the process certainly reduced the numbers flying around the living and kitchen areas.

When we had marched into Changi I suppose it would be fair to say that we all were about as rich as each other. We had not had a pay-day for a long time and I would guess that the average cash held in the pocket was not more than ten dollars each. That was the sum paid to me each week from 17-10-41 until 24-01-42, as recorded in my old AB 64 (Army Service Book and Pay Book), and there was no incentive for any of us to save. However, it was not long before the majority of pockets were empty while a few were more than full. The reason appeared to be that there were four main groups of prisoners, quite irrespective of race, unit or rank. First, there were a few who risked their lives to go through the wire and to bring back black market materials which they then sold at high prices commensurate with the risks taken. Classified in terms of cash in pocket, these few were the wealthy ones, In fact I knew of some who were accepting gold rings and undated cheques.

Second was a larger number who, while not being prepared to go out at night and risk being shot at by the Japs or, more likely by the Sikh guards, nevertheless were not happy to be idle. They worked hard at some sort of trade, making things to sell, and were a rather poor 'middle class' who, while not being completely indigent, could never have been called wealthy. They may, perhaps, have been the happiest and the most likely to survive. Boredom was a great danger, giving a chance for a feeling of hopelessness and the belief that one would 'never get off the island'. I saw men who, although ill, were cheerfully carrying on their trade, while there were others, not basically ill, who died in their sleep because they could not think of a reason for getting up to face another day. The third group represented the bulk of the prisoners who were not prepared to take the risks attached to the black market, and not determined enough to attempt some honest trade. In my grouping they would have to be the 'undeserving poor'.

The fourth group were those who in the normal circumstances might have been in any one of the first three groups but who in fact were in hospital and probably in greater need of extras than the rest of us, but with no chance of taking action to obtain them. They were generally rated as the 'deserving poor'.

In those early days in Changi I was one of the artisans, making tobacco pipes out of bamboo, and also making sewing needles from corned beef can keys. I tried to make drinking mugs from cut-down glass bottles but I never really mastered the cutting business so that I wasted the raw materials and consequently was out of pocket on that venture. I was grateful to the black marketeers because they were my only supply of such things as tobacco, cigars, gula malacca (a brown sugar made from the sap of the Nipa palm), salt, chillis and oil - coconut and red palm.

It was not many weeks before the great majority had no money at all and so were completely dependent upon the official rations from the cookhouse, such as they were, and had no honest access to luxuries like those I have just listed. Nobody thought to do much about that state of affairs but then, on behalf of the 'deserving poor' in the hospitals, the senior officers in Changi made an attempt to 'nationalise' the black market, putting the traders on a salary so that a decent percentage of the takings could go to the welfare of the sick. The idea sounded fine and it seemed to work for a short time, until it became apparent that, with the big profit removed, the black marketeers were no longer prepared to take the risks involved. The scheme collapsed, but after a short delay, the traders began to go through the wire once more, some but not all making a voluntary contribution to the hospitals. That is what I saw and understood in Birdwood Camp, but there could have been a very different outcome in other areas, such as among the Australians. For that first two months I was never outside my own area.

CHAPTER FIVE

THE GREAT WORLD

After a few weeks in Birdwood, our cooks learned the proper way to cook rice and so the quality of our basic diet improved a little. As a result, our hemispherical abdomens began to subside and the frequency of visits to the urinal dropped back to only a little above normal. Unfortunately, however, the quantity of rice was never sufficient and we were deplorably short of other foods and vitamins. Deficiency diseases were beginning to appear but at that early stage they were not fully recognised. Some private cooking helped a little but this was only for those who were able to obtain the extra food. Although my handicrafts earned me a little money, or food by direct barter, I was beginning to feel permanently hungry and would listen with envy when I heard rather vague stories of men on working parties in Singapore who were able to obtain all kinds of goodies. I began to wish that I too could go to Singapore.

My chance came on the 15th May 1942 when, with Douglas Polley, I joined a party of about a hundred men of the 155 under the leadership of Capt. R.G. Coles, with three subalterns: Tinsley, Legard and Douglas-Home. In a small fleet of trucks with Australian drivers we were taken to 'The Great World' amusement park at the top of the Havelock Road. Apparently there were two other similar amusement parks: 'The Happy World' and 'The New World', although I saw only the one. We were told that before the coming of the Japanese, all three had been very popular with the local inhabitants.

The Great World occupied an area of about four acres and its entrance near the road junction was a tall gateway, made of a timber frame covered with flat and painted sheets of galvanised steel, shaped like an ornamental *pai lu* or Chinese gateway. On each side of the entrance were two lions, male and female, like those often to be seen outside the entrances to Chinese temples and other public buildings. Within the park a roadway about thirty feet wide ran in the shape of a big O-shaped loop and on each side were eating houses, games stalls, souvenir shops, fortune tellers' booths and a roundabout for children. At the eastern end, not far from the gateway but within the loop of the roadway, was a nicely laid out tea garden, now being used by the camp doctors. Just inside the gateway and hard round to the left was a brick building which served as the Japanese guardroom. Beyond it, on both sides of the road were a group of similar single-storey brick buildings, in one of which Douglas and I later lived. Apart from these few, every other structure was built like the gateway, of timber frames covered with flat galvanised sheets Most of them still had the garish painted decoration of the park's heyday but by the time I saw it the place was looking very dingy.

When our party arrived we found that all the buildings and stalls except for a few at the far or western end were occupied by Australians and we had difficulty in finding accommodation. The best that Douglas and I could find was two wooden trestle tables under the circular roof of the children's roundabout. The result was that we were soaked every time it rained at night. This bothered me at first but soon we grew accustomed to it and came to little harm. Of course we were never cold and it was only necessary to spread out whatever bedding one had before leaving in the morning and, on most days, it would be quite dry and sweet smelling by the time we returned in the evening.

A wooden table is not a very comfortable bed. I think Douglas found a car cushion, but I had nothing and slept hard for a few nights until, one evening, exploring in a battered and unoccupied building at the extreme western end, I found a big ball of thick string. Immediately I thought of a hammock, but there was nowhere from which I could hang one if I made it. However, continuing my exploration, I found a very battered wardrobe, with its base as a separate unit. The base was four feet long and eighteen inches wide, and quite sturdily constructed, and I soon realised that it would do as a bed. I released it and carried it back in triumph to my table. The next job, which took three days, was to make a net to fit the base frame. In use my shoulders and hips were on the net while my head was on a pillow made up of underclothes on top of my big pack, and my feet rested on an old beer crate. As a bed it came far short of normal standards but was a vast improvement over the bare table top, and at the end of a hard day's work I slept well enough, even when it rained.

After one day of settling in we then discovered the reason for our presence in Singapore town. We were to become something like stevedores; humping, sorting and stacking the large quantity of merchandise that was lying in the docks. After our fighting forces had been on Singapore island for a few days it became obvious that capitulation in some form was inevitable. There were many ships in the harbour and we heard that they were being emptied and would be used to evacuate the defending troops. Of course this never happened, although we heard later that a number of women and children had got away. Having no say in such matters, I and my friends just shrugged our shoulders, but I am sure we should have felt guilty if we had just left the Singaporeans to face the Japanese alone while we escaped. Anyway, the ships, having dumped all their cargoes higgledy-piggledy into the godowns (warehouses), sailed away empty.

The mass bombing had made an almost indescribable mess of the mixed merchandise which had been dumped by the ships, and it was our job to provide the labour to sort it out and to cart it to other godowns, ready for the Japanese. Each morning began with a parade of all the workers and a roll call outside the guardroom, but the Nips were never very thorough at taking the count or of checking the numbers of sick as quoted by the two Australian doctors. We were then split into small groups and marched by a Nip soldier to our place of work. My first job, which lasted for three days, was in a quayside godown somewhere in Keppel Harbour, where we found a large number of jumbled up heavy packing cases. Our party of about ten men had to collect these as directed by the Nip soldier and manhandle them across the warehouse to a large rope net spread on the floor near the main door and under an overhead crane. Then a truck, driven by an Aussie prisoner, was backed into the godown, the crane lifted the loaded net, and we had then to arrange and stack the cases on the truck.

It was at this early stage that I first understood what was probably our biggest problem: that of communication. The Nips knew only a few words of English while the prisoners, with one or two rare exceptions, knew not one word of Japanese. Our Nip had selected the cases which he wanted us to move and indicated them by pointing and, when the net was full and ready to be lifted, he called up to the crane driver, an Aussie: 'OK-ka'. The Aussie, thinking that 'OK-ka', spoken almost without inflection, was Japanese for: 'I'm all right' or 'I'm ready', replied similarly: 'OK-ka.' How was he, new to the job, to know that the Nip had asked a question: 'Are you all right?' This exchange was repeated once or twice until the Nip, thinking that the Aussie was 'taking the mickey', or whatever they call it in Japan, climbed up the ladder and out to the crane, where he took a swipe at the Aussie's head. The Aussie swayed away to avoid the blow, lost his balance, fell off his lofty perch and severely damaged his ankle. That ended the transporting business for the day because none of the party knew, or would admit to knowing, how to drive the crane. The same sort of thing happened many times, presumably all over the town, and many a POW took a good clout, only to ask: 'And what the hell was that for?' And all of that quite widespread trouble arose because nobody told us that the suffix -ka denotes a question.

Amongst the assorted stuff in that part of the docks there must have been a cargo of dyestuffs and one of the drums must have had its contents blown all around the district. I identified it as a black powder which was not noticeable as it lay like a dust on the boxes and crates, but as soon as our sweaty bodies came in contact with it we were stained. For more than a week dozens of other prisoners and myself were walking around with our bodies patchily dyed to a vivid reddish-purple. Our strange appearance evoked a few laughs and ribald remarks from the local people as we marched back to camp but, over all the time, we never received anything but kindness and sympathy from them. About two weeks after I went to The Great World a well-educated Chinese gentleman told me that we had done the right thing when we stayed in Singapore instead of sailing away in the ships. What effect that decision had on longer-term attitudes and the path of history I really don't know, but apparently it helped us. Often, when our working parties were marching back to camp in the evening, one or two of the locals, perhaps small boys but also elderly men and women, would note the position of the Nip escort and then go round to the opposite side of the column and slip quickly in between the files of prisoners. There they would grin and hand over one or more small offerings of food before disappearing among the other people on the pavement.

I spent three days humping cement and for me that job was really heavy work. The 1-cwt (50 kilos) bags were brought to the inland warehouse on a big truck, and we had to move and stack them in the warehouse. The bags were lifted up by two men on the truck and then dropped onto the shoulders of the other men as they passed below the rear of the high truck. We then had to carry them across the pavement, across a yard and to the far end of a long warehouse, where we had to walk up a steeply-sloping plank and stack them on a large and growing pile. I calculated that in those three days I must have had nearly eighteen tons of cement dropped onto the back of my neck. It was very hard work, and my neck vertebrae have never been right since.

Another humping job which, happily for me, I missed was with bags of caustic soda. According to the description given by my friends, the work was very similar to that with the cement except that whereas I had bruised and sore neck and shoulders, most of those carrying the caustic soda had very severe burns. I saw some of those wounds and would expect that the men's scars would be there till the end of their days.

On another day we were taken to an inland shed in which were a number of absolutely huge sacks which seemed to be far too large for us to lift. However, when we tried we were surprised to find that they were very light indeed. The sacks were full of dried spices but while they were light and smelled rather pleasant, the dust from them soon became well rubbed into our perspiring skins. The red chillis were probably the worst but whatever the cause, we all soon had bright scarlet and inflamed shoulders, arms and backs, and once again there was a long queue at the evening sick parade.

Quite apart from the damage and hurt caused by the carrying of noxious materials, all the prisoners were very prone to skin diseases. As soldiers most of us had been afflicted with vegetable or fungal parasites such as ringworm or tinea, but in our debilitated state and with the shortage of vitamins, as prisoners we suffered from a wide variety of skin troubles. Even a simple sweat rash could, and often did, turn septic. The crotch, the waistline and the armpits were the most commonly afflicted areas. Our doctors did their best but they had pitifully few drugs and medicines.

In The Great World there was apparently a fair supply of three medicaments: yellow Acriflavine, red Mercurochrome, and purple Gentian Violet. I didn't know the specific uses of any of these, but apparently our two Australian doctors did. At every evening sick parade there would be a long queue of men wearing only shorts and a pair of wooden, Chinese-style sandals. As each man came up, the doctor would examine the sores and then specify a colour; yellow, red, or violet.

The man would then join the appropriate one of three queues where three medical orderlies sat on a low bench. On the floor between each orderly's feet was a big bowl of the dye. Whenever he saw a pair of sandalled feet appear before him, suddenly to be covered by a rather grubby pair of shorts, he would wield a large camel-hair paint brush and anoint the affected areas, never having time to raise his eyes above the affected part. I remember ribbing one of the Australian orderlies by suggesting that in years to come his young son would ask: 'And what did you do in the war, Daddy?, and he, being a truthful man, would then have to reply: 'I painted men's Tea Things violet!' (or red, or yellow as the case may be). Sometimes, a man would require decoration with more than one colour and in the early days, when these were combined with the cyclamen coloured dye stains mentioned earlier the overall effects were quite startling and many a Red Indian brave might have envied us.

I spent four days at an inland group of sheds where the work was to carry rough-sawn boxes of Sunlight Soap from one shed to another. Although the boxes were quite heavy, I felt cheerful because Port Sunlight, where the soap was made, is quite near to where my home was at that time. In a peculiar way the words printed on the boxes acted as a link with the familiar things of pre-war days, The work was clean and not dangerous; nor was it as arduous as some of the chores I had been given but, as usual, there was a snag. Working stripped to the waist, our stomachs were soon scratched and filled with small splinters from the rough wooden boxes. I became slightly less fond of Billy Lever and his heirs and successors and muttered a lot as, back at my billet, I tried to extract splinters from around my navel.

The work in that particular group of warehouses was not of great interest, but one thing has stuck in my memory. On all my earlier jobs and on most that came later, the Japanese soldier guards spoke no English and made no attempt to communicate with us beyond the need to direct our work and urge us to greater speed.

Here, however, one of the Japanese was a middle-aged and studious-looking man, much less muscular than most of those already seen, and he tried to practise his modest knowledge of the English language when giving his orders. Also, he demonstrated a little kindness and sympathy which was truly exceptional. One day at about noon he called in a quiet voice: 'Stoppu! Oru men come here!' We then saw that he had a large white enamelled can containing some milk which he had made by mixing the contents of several cans of sweetened condensed milk with water. He waved us away to: 'Koppu buringu' (bring cup) and then dished out a teacup full of his 'miruku' to each of us. When all had received a cup of milk and muttered a word of thanks, most of the men moved away, but I hung back and spoke to our benefactor. I thanked him for his kindness and asked his name, hoping that we might attempt a little conversation, but he suddenly appeared to be very shy. For some reason he did not want the other Nips on the site to see him fraternising. He muttered what I took to be his name, smiled briefly and waved me away and back to the work. The name sounded like 'Naka C. K.' and that is how I have remembered him although, with much later knowledge, it was probably 'Nakashiike', a rather uncommon Japanese family name. On two more days he called: 'Oru men come here!' and in addition to the milk, he handed to each of us two British-made sweet biscuits out of a decorated box. On the second day of receiving the biscuits I walked away to eat them in the shade round the corner of a hut. Hardly had I done so when another Nip came round the far corner and walked up to me. Seeing the biscuits, he challenged me with a few unintelligible but aggressive-sounding words. Then he too tried some English: 'Who givu ka'. I did not want to 'snitch' on one who could be called a friend but after only a moment of thought it was clear that there was no point in making things difficult. 'Naka C. K.'

I said, whereupon the aggressive Nip stopped his snarling and laughed as if it was a great joke - which I did not understand. He repeated the name: 'Naka She Kay', laughed again and with an 'Ush. OK!' he walked away. 'Strange folk, these Nips!', I thought. I never saw our kindly, milk-giving Nip again but the fact that I have remembered him over all the years must indicate something.

With the exception of the Sunlight Soap, none of the merchandise I have so far described was of much interest to the prisoners, but when working in other godowns which contained a more varied stock, we soon discovered that some of the things were potentially of great value to us. Before the arrival of the Japanese, many commodities in general use in Singapore and Malaya were imported, coming mostly from the United Kingdom. Now, of course, the imports had stopped and we were handling virtually the only stocks of those materials. And truly various they were. More than once I heard the POW boast: 'You name it; I've handled it.' One of the first commodities that came to my notice was cotton sewing thread, usually to be found as a dozen wooden reels packed in a paper wrapper. These were rather bulky but yet I and many others managed to smuggle them out of the warehouses. There were many other small items which were comparatively easy to conceal, including. sewing machine needles, ordinary needles, loose false teeth, lipsticks, propelling pencils, fountain pens, buttons, steel tools, packets of steel nuts and bolts, screws and so on. An incidental matter of surprise and envy was that while we, the British POWs, were taking the sewing machine needles, the Australians, who provided almost all of the truck drivers, took the machines.

Our first inclination was to take canned food, of which there was a lot lying around, but although food was always our prime target we soon discovered that there were better ways of obtaining it. If we took any of the many items already mentioned, these could be sold to the Chinese 'black market' traders for money which would buy, perhaps from the same man, far more food than we could carry or conceal. Thus, when the Chinese people slipped into our ranks after the early days they were carrying not food but paper dollars to exchange for our smuggled goods.

Quite soon after our arrival in The Great World, the Japanese guard allowed one or two Chinese traders to set up a food stall in the roadway just to the side of the guardroom. The bartering was done by the men at the front, well screened by a press of others behind so that, at least ostensibly, the guard commander did not know what was going on. However, he was not a fool and so, every evening, usually after the pushing crowd of prisoners had subsided a little, he would go straight to the far end of the long trestle counter, where the senior Chinese trader would silently hand over a large box packed with canned food and a few English cigarettes. Away went the guard commander with his 'perks', and the illicit trading proceeded without further hindrance.

When a case of marketable and transportable goods was found in a godown, word would be passed around and then, intermittently, men would go singly and unobtrusively to the case and by repeated attack would open the case sufficiently to allow a hand in. The articles stolen were then cached elsewhere in the godown, ready to be concealed on the prisoner's person shortly before departure time. They were then sold after a quick haggle on the road, or were carried back to the traders in the camp. There were a few men in each party who, for reasons of shyness or lack of dexterity, were complete bunglers, and of course they were a great danger to the rest of us. However, the majority became very expert at the smuggling game and there were few accidents. If a real duffer was with a party he was firmly told to lay off and often would be given a percentage of cash when we got back to camp.

I recall one typical incident when, in a party of about twenty men, I had been working in a godown beside the Singapore River, on Robertson Quay and with the Havelock Road high above us on the far side of the river. The day was done and we had formed up in three ranks in the roadway, ready to march back to camp. The Nip *gunso* (sergeant) had counted us and was just about to give the command to march when a *heitai* (private soldier) ran shouting out of the godown. It was obvious that he had found signs that something had been taken. The gunso gestured to the British sergeant leading our party and the order was given: 'Open order - march! Remove caps!' We went through the manoeuvre smartly enough and those who had them removed their caps. The *gunso* and his two soldiers then went down the ranks, looking in the caps and haversacks and at the contents of all turned out pockets. Nothing was found so the gunso gestured again,: 'Remove shirts! Remove socks!' Once again the Nips went down the ranks and once again they found nothing. They were puzzled but far from satisfied, and conferred among themselves for several minutes while we, standing barefoot and wearing only our trousers, grumbled audibly. At last there was more gesticulation and the final order was given.

There in a street in Singapore and in full view of the busy main road above, some twenty British soldiers dropped their trousers, and underpants if they had them, and bent over to expose their bare backsides to the amused gaze of the numerous passers-by. The Nips went along the ranks for the third time, looking carefully if not gently, and still they found nothing. Our sergeant told us to dress up and to close ranks but as soon as we were once again ready to march, the gunso demanded open order once more. The two *heitai* then went down the ranks and each prisoner received four swinging blows to the side of the jaw: a left and a right from each of them. Our sergeant was lucky; he received just two blows, delivered personally by the *gunso*. I think they knew we had beaten them and the bashing was just to save face. Eventually, and about half an hour late, we marched away and back up the Havelock Road to our camp, whistling 'Colonel Bogey' as loudly as possible. Arrived at the camp, we all unloaded our spoils. As a typical example, I had two half-gross packets (144 in all) of ten-inch hacksaw blades which later were sold for a good price and kept me and Douglas eating reasonably well for about a week. There was a time when the secret of how it was done was to be guarded, but now, after so long, I'll tell you. The trick depended upon the clothes we wore.

As prisoners, the 'bucket' shorts were always worn down and, if possible, in a larger size than normal so that the bottoms came down to the ankles. They made us look like very scruffy cartoon sailors, but who cared? The hosetops were worn with the lower ends inside the socks and they were tied with string at both top and bottom. Articles to be smuggled were tucked inside the hosetops, on the inside front of the shin, and so that the baggy trousers would hang clear and look normal. During a search the boots and socks could be removed without touching the hose tops, and when the trousers had to be lowered, they were held at just below the knee so that, while bare feet protruded, the hosetops and their contents were invisible, concealed by the bunched trouser legs. However, the most important requirement was the ability to keep a straight face!

Soon after arriving at a big warehouse in the harbour, a rather tall and slender Nip of about thirty-five came up to me. He was wearing a smart light khaki coloured bush jacket and matching well-pressed trousers. He wore no hat or badges but was carrying a foolscap-sized note pad. With a very slight bow he asked in passably good English if I would please go with him and led the way to a large pile of sacks in a corner. Pointing to a sack which had been opened, he asked if I could tell him what it contained. I took a handful of whitish and lumpy-looking crystals and examined them closely, noting a very faint smell of ammonia. There were no marks on the sacks but the stuff looked very like ammonium nitrate, doubtless imported as a concentrated fertiliser. However, even in those days I remembered enough school chemistry to know that ammonium nitrate could be used as an explosive. Even though the man was very pleasant and did say 'please', there was no need to tell him such a thing. Hoping that he would not recognise the difference in crystal shape, I took his pencil and wrote NH_3SO_4. He immediately named it as ammonium sulphate, also a fertiliser but not explosive; and then he looked very surprised, not at the nature of the material but at the fact that I had been able to identify it.

He quickly made a note on his pad but then smilingly asked a few questions about me, all related to pre-war days. As on an earlier occasion, some conversation would have been interesting but caution indicated that we should part as quickly as possible, so I excused myself and rejoined the other men of the working party.

I cannot remember what we were sorting out on that particular day but in the process I found a well made and varnished wooden box of about a foot cube in size. The lid had only a snap-catch and inside was an optical instrument which looked like a gun sight except for the fact that its objective lens pointed downward. I guessed that it must be some kind of bomb sight and so, with two or three covert visits, I managed to remove the eye-piece and put it in my pocket. Then, while we were resting for a few minutes after eating our lunch, it was dropped quietly into the dock.

Almost at the end of the same day I found on the floor behind some cases a slightly torn and dirty cardboard box of cigarette papers containing, I think, some two hundred little packets. When going out of the godown I showed it to one of our Nip guards and asked if I might have it. 'Presento-ka?' was by then the accepted word. Obviously in a hurry to be finished and away, he grabbed the box and looked quickly at the contents, gave me one hard clout and then stuffed the box in my haversack. As cigarettes were difficult to obtain but tobacco, of various and sometimes dubious quality, was reasonably available, most cigarette smokers rolled their own. Suitably thin paper was not so easily found and it is sad to say that many Bibles and prayer books, printed on thin India paper, ended up in smoke. That box of real cigarette papers was a great boon to me and a few of my friends and lasted for several months.

I spent two days in a very scruffy looking warehouse beside a small river, exact location now forgotten. Its main content was a big pile of copra (dried coconut kernel from which coconut oil is obtained), which we had to shovel into sacks. At the other end of the long and narrow shed were several very battered bales of tobacco leaf and a lot of loose leaves lying on the floor.

My boots and shorts smelled of that nearly rancid copra for weeks afterwards, but a consoling feature was that the smell reminded me of the oil and cake mills at Port Sunlight, which I had passed twice a day as I cycled to and from school, oh, so very long ago.

However, always with the opportunist's eye, my main interest was in the tobacco leaf and I was able to select several sweet smelling and nicely flexible leaves and to store them in my haversack.

There was no search that day, and no difficulty in carrying them back to camp. Eventually, and taking advice from some Australian friends, the leaves were well-moistened with a sticky solution of gula malacca, bought from the Chinese trader, and some rum; and for the life of me I cannot remember where I found that. Then I rolled the lot into a tight bundle, wrapped it in a piece of clean rag and tied it up with some coarse string. The bundle was then put between two pieces of board and wedged tightly under my bed frame, where it stayed for several weeks. Eventually, when shavings were sliced off the end and wrapped in my 'pukka' papers, it made a beautiful cigarette and kept me smoking for a long time.

My remembered experience of stevedoring, with its allied activities of thieving and smuggling, and its associated hard work, sweat and general anguish, was common to all the prisoners who went out form The Great World and other similar places in the town. However, I have other and more personal memories of that time, almost all of them happy. I mentioned earlier that there was an open-air cinema in The Great World. Soon after arriving there we discovered that the Aussies were using it as a theatre and there were two shows each week. On Saturdays there was a concert and on Wednesdays there was 'book and poetry reading', which was really a news briefing. I saw the concert on our first Saturday evening in camp and then sought out its producer: Australian Sergeant Major Sonny Lloyd. Telling him briefly of my interest in theatre, I volunteered to help with the next production. With a big smile, Sonny immediately invited me to 'join the show, Cobber'; and then introduced me to one or two other Australians who were the mainstays of the concert party. The one I remember best was Sergeant John French who was the stage electrician. He and I got on very well together.

It would not be unfair to say that at that time the camp concert was a rather amateur affair. There were several people with good and bright ideas for sketches and other items but the staging of them was poor. The design, construction and painting of sets was almost non-existent, while the lighting facilities were minimal. Thinking that all of those things could be improved, perhaps I boasted a little, but Sonny and John encouraged me, as did Captain Bill Rook who had a background in broadcasting. When I first saw the stage it was very small, consisting of a simple box about thirty feet wide and twenty feet high, in the front of which was an opening or proscenium arch about twenty feet wide and twelve feet high, fitted with a pair of draw curtains on a good sliding track. Unfortunately, the stage was only nine feet deep from curtain to back wall, and I complained to Sonny that it was too small to allow of ` any interesting scenery behind the acting area. Typical of the Australians, within the week and before the next show, the front wall, curtain and all, had been moved forward by four feet, and a dressing room had been built at the side.

The lighting was very primitive but John and I searched the camp, and while all the lower wattage lamp bulbs were in use in the various billets, we found several high wattage lamps: 300, 500, and 1,000 watt, and these were mounted into 4-gallon petrol cans to make very useful flood lights. I found at the back of the camp a disused neon sign workshop containing a generous supply of coloured glass tubing which, when suitably mounted, made colour filters to fit over the big light boxes. I made eight water-dimmers out of some one-inch glass tubing, bent into a U-shape over a primus stove, and John made a frame of levers with which to work them. We wired up the new stage as best we could, and soon we had a really workable theatre.

Incidentally, the time to do all that work came by courtesy of our two kindly and very co-operative Australian doctors, who wrote us off as 'sick' for the time required. They continued to do this for me throughout the time I was in The Great World and, fortunately for them as well as me, the Japanese guards never checked the numbers of sick against actual names. As the auditorium was large enough to seat every man in the camp, each show was staged on just the one Saturday evening, and thus I was rarely out on a working party on the Friday, that being the day when I rigged the stage for the next show.

Not long after we started working together, John French asked where my billet was and when told that Douglas and I slept on two tables without any shelter he suggested that we should move in with him and his brother. Three Aussie sergeants lived in a brick building just round the corner from the guardroom, and they made Douglas and me feel very welcome. I untied my string net and brought it with me but, although I planned for the worst, in fact it was never needed again.

I really enjoyed the designing, making and painting of colourful settings for the bigger items in our programmes. The aim always was to provide a setting, usually for a musical number, which would evoke memories of happier days far from the Pacific. Here I boast that on several occasions men came to me after a show, not so much to congratulate as to say thanks for a few minutes of mental transportation. All the scenes were studied and criticised and in one purporting to be a hotel balcony overlooking a bay somewhere on the French Riviera, two gunners were much impressed by a great and curving bay with the lights on the promenade fading away into the distance. They were rather disappointed as mathematicians when they learned that there was just a single bulb in a long, white-painted box and that the lights for which they were trying to calculate the wattages were really a line of holes punched in a cut out piece of currugated cardboard.

On one or two occasions I provided a turn for the Wednesday evenings, between readings of the news. I played tangos on the piano, being billed as 'Cuban Pete', and wrote two or three short mystery or ghost stories which, unseen, I read over the amplifier. On Saturday nights, however, the stage demanded my full attention.

Some of the items devised by Sonny and others were quite ambitious and sometimes called for a lot of good costumes, both male and female. Some of the men, mostly Australians, were good at playing female parts although none could provide a soprano voice. Still, we did our best and sometimes could have as many as ten men and ten 'women', or even more, in full evening dress. The clothes were brought into camp in ones and twos when they were found, usually in the warehouses in the town. They had belonged to the managers and wives of the various trading companies, and mostly were found in the 'bird cages', the locked areas where valuable or un-bonded goods were stored. The Nip soldiers had broken in and opened all the suitcases, probably with a bayonet. Presumably, they had taken any valuables but had left the clothes.

Gekijo (theatre) was one of the first Japanese words I learned, and when these clothes were found they were taken to the Nip guard with the words: '*Gekijo presento-ka*'. Usually there was no trouble other than the customary open handed clout to the side of the jaw, but this we reckoned as fair payment and the clothes were carried back in triumph to the theatre. The Japanese guards in the warehouses thought we were quite mad, but not so those in our camp nor, indeed, many of the senior officers of the Imperial Japanese Army (IJA). Every Saturday evening we had to keep the front two rows of seats for them, and on most occasions these were filled with high ranking Japanese officers, and their interpreter, whose name was Fuji.

After one show, the final curtain call had been taken and the applause had not quite died away when I heard the clump and clank of boots and swords on the steps coming up to the front of the stage. Then I heard Fuji's voice calling:

'Suteiji maneijah! Suteiji Maneijah!'. 'Hell!' I thought. 'What have I done now?' I was wearing only a loin cloth and a pair of canvas plimsols and felt in no way properly attired to have to face up to an irate Nip General in full dress and complete with sword. As the footsteps came up onto the apron-stage I noticed that everyone else had hurried off, except John who stayed by his switchboard. Fuji pushed through the centre opening and after I had given the curtain rope a quick tug I moved rather reluctantly towards him. He was followed by five or six officers, all middle aged, and with their big swords swinging and clanking behind them. Feeling very vulnerable in my near nudity, I was not quite sure what to do so I just stood to attention and waited. Fuji asked in his rather lisping voice: 'Are you the stage manager? 'Yes,' I replied and glanced around me, hoping for some help. Then I noticed faces peeping round the wings and other pieces of scenery. The other men had crept back, and their half-seen faces looked just as apprehensive as I felt.

'The General' (Yamashita), said Fuji, 'wishes to compliment you on the show. He thinks it was very clever.'

'Oh, er – thank you.'

And I turned towards the Japanese, who appeared to be the eldest and had the most decoration on his dark green uniform. To my surprise he extended his hand, shook mine, and bowed to me. Not knowing what to do, I bowed back and was immediately aware of an audible sigh of relief from the players now gathered in the wings. Fuji then said that they would like to meet the company and inspect the stage so I introduced Sonny Lloyd, rather pleased that as he had not been playing a part, he too was almost naked.

While Sonny and the General were exchanging bows and a few words via the interpreter, I beckoned to the company to get into line, and Sonny introduced them all in turn. Then all the visitors inspected the stage, being intrigued by the switchboard which John demonstrated. They looked at my bits of scenery, smiling and commenting to each other when they saw the old rubbish out of which it was made.

Then one of the visitors noticed the amplifier and microphone which was tucked into a corner behind the proscenium arch. Fuji asked, 'What is zis?' and I fancied there was a touch of suspicion in his voice. Sonny quickly replied that it was the amplifier, and pointed up to the loudspeaker hanging over the centre of the proscenium. He switched it on and blew on the microphone so that the noise could be heard. Fuji, still suspicious, asked where was the aerial and was quickly assured that there was no aerial; it was only a simple amplifier. Several pairs of Japanese eyes peered at the untidy collection of valves and transformers but eventually appeared to be satisfied. In fact the receiver parts, whereby Sonny got his Wednesday evening news, were well hidden below the stage and reasonably safe. In fact I never saw them. After much clicking of their heels, followed by bows to and from those of us still on the stage, the officers stomped and clanked down the steps and away. Fuji hung back to tell me that the General was very pleased and thought our theatre produced the best entertainment in Singapore.

The Concert Party had a small committee which met frequently, usually in Bill Rook's billet, to discuss ideas for coming shows, and it was decided that on Saturday, 16th August 1942 we should put on a 'memorial' show to mark six months since the end of the fighting. There was some demur about the use of the Union Flag and the National Anthem because both of these had been banned by the IJA. However, much as the result of the visit by General Yamashita, we decided to go ahead.

The first half of the show was a mix of concert party turns and sketches, all of them more or less humorous and light, but the second half was all one item dedicated to the memory of our fallen comrades. I designed a set which had, upstage and to the audience's right, a bier draped with a Union Flag, and at its corners were to stand four soldiers on guard. At the back of the stage was a black curtain up which rose, from behind the bier and diagonally to the top on the left hand side, a diverging 'searchlight beam' of white-painted cardboard. High up in its broad part was a black silhouette map of the Malayan peninsula, and on it were a number of small Latin crosses, about three inches high and covered with glittering tinfoil to represent the sites of all the battles.

The scene opened with our pianist playing Handel's *Dead March* in *Saul*, and here I must apologise and admit that for the life of me I cannot remember his name. He was an excellent concert party pianist and we relied on him, not only to provide whatever music was required but also to give cues and introductions, always exactly as rehearsed.

After a few bars the curtains opened slowly to reveal the scene, with four soldiers on guard with their heads bowed over their reversed rifles (made from scrap wood). Slowly changing coloured lights illuminated the searchlight beam, a bright white spot lit the bier, and a separate trio of coloured lights shone on a four foot high 'solid' cross down-stage on the left. Then, without any audible commands but in meticulous slow time to the tempo of the music, a sergeant marched in with four more soldiers, all carrying rifles at the slope. Still without audible command, they proceeded to change the guard, this being done really well, including all the reversing of the weapons, the outstretching of the soldiers' arms and the final bowing of the heads. After a pause while the music finished, an Australian entered and stood beside the cross and, lit by another white spotlight, recited his own poem: 'Cobbers – We Will Remember Them'. Finally the piano sounded loudly the introduction to the National Anthem. I could see through a spy hole that the whole audience, including the Japanese officers in the front two rows, immediately stood to attention. The whole concert party, all out of sight behind the black curtains, then sang 'God Save The King' as loudly as possible, joined immediately by the audience. The Japanese officers came to the salute and held it until the curtain closed. There was great applause but there were no curtain calls.

Lt. Tinsley of the 155 provided the eight men and a sergeant, and I know that they spent many evening hours rehearsing and drilling for the changing of the guard. They wore smart British uniforms that had been borrowed from among their fellow gunners and, just to provide a united appearance, they wore Australian felt hats.

The resulting presentation was beyond praise and I felt very proud of my fellow gunners; the more so because I could see how much their performance had impressed the Japanese officers.

Shortly after the Memorial show, Lt. Tinsley offered to write and to produce a complete show, drawing all his cast from the 155. It was staged about four weeks later, its theme being of an artillery regiment in action against some enemy, unspecified but clearly not Japanese. The script was rather unrefined but it moved well and was full of humorous quips. They poked fun at many things but particularly at the Army's ideas of 'bull', and also at old Indian 'pukka sahibs', of whom we had all met a few. When the battle started, with much off-stage noise of bangs, shouting and the distant rattle of machine guns, the Colonel, after spluttering over his drink with a visitor, announced that he must just go to the privy. The noise of battle continued as several men came in singly with messages for the Colonel, all being told by the RSM, using signs only, of his present whereabouts and condition. Then came the unmistakeable throbbing whistle of a howitzer shell coming in, followed by an enormous bang as the shell landed on a certain small building nearby.

Lt. Tinsley offered his script and asked if we could provide the bang. He was pleased and surprised when I said that, by a happy coincidence, I thought it might be possible.

A few weeks earlier, when working in a town warehouse, I had found some black powder, used for re-filling shot gun cartridges, and had smuggled three of the little celluloid containers back to camp. Now, when a good stage bomb was wanted, a little experimentation was needed. I took half the contents of one little box and wrapped it in thin paper, including two wires and a suitable fuse. The small ball was then wrapped in insulation tape and string to make it the size of a golf ball. It looked about right and similar to ones bought and used twice in University days, but the need to test it remained.

One Friday afternoon when I was alone in the billet the test was made. The bomb was wired to the mains and put in a large steel drum like a dustbin, which was then placed in a corner and well away from personal belongings. I looked outside and there was nobody about so I went back in and closed the switch. There was an enormous bang, very satisfactory indeed and, to my delight, not to mention a little surprise, there was no sign of damage anywhere. I was just about to roll myself a cigarette when I heard running footsteps and two of the guards dashed past the door. I called and beckoned to them to come in, which they did in silence but with obvious suspicion. One kept his rifle very obviously pointed at me. They knew about our theatre and often watched the show from by the entrance so I quickly used the magic word *gekijo* and explained by signs that in eight days time a similar bomb would be used on the stage. They were both invited to see the show. The pointing rifle was moved to the 'port' position and both Nips began to laugh. I heaved a sigh of relief and ushered them to the door before they could ask embarrassing questions about the source of the explosive.

The following Saturday, with the usual two front rows of Japanese officers, the new bomb, with three-quarters of a packet of black powder, was in its bin at the back of the stage. As the cue for the whole cast to whistle was given, I peeped through my spy hole, my left hand out behind me to cue John to fire the bomb.

To my surprise the whole audience ducked down in response to the familiar sound, and when the bomb exploded with a very satisfactory bang, everyone disappeared! A second later, they all sat up again and there was a roar of laughter, followed by sustained clapping and it was some time before the show could continue, to reveal that there had been a direct hit on the privy, Colonel included. I fully expected another invasion from the IJA but none came. However, next morning, Sunday, I had a second visit from the two Nip guards who, full of grins, indicated that the show had been very good - and gave me a packet of cigarettes!

At the end of August 1942 we were ordered by the IJA to sign a promise not to attempt escape, but naturally the men in The Great World refused to do so. Nothing more was heard until the 7th September when the papers were again presented and we were told that everyone in Changi had signed. There were rumours, later confirmed, that they had done so under extreme duress, 16,000 men having been crammed into the Selarang Barracks which had been designed for a maximum of 850 men. With thousands of men, many of them sick, huddled in the open barrack square and with machine guns trained on them all the time, they held out for four days and only agreed to sign when the Japanese Commander, Colonel Fukue, threatened to bring in the men from the hospitals.

There was some quick discussion, and many signed with fictitious names or the name of someone else. I wrote 'N.D. Polley' and Douglas wrote 'P.S. Rhodes', and others wrote 'Donald Duck'or 'Mickey Mouse'. It was rather a futile act but at least we could maintain that the names on our forms were forgeries. The Japanese commanders responsible for the Selarang Incident were sentenced to death by the War Crimes Commission in 1946.

The Japanese supplied meagre rations of rice and vegetables, all prepared by our British or Australian cooks. However, almost everyone did their own cooking of extras, made mostly from the canned foods we bought from the Chinese traders. The usual form was as 'rissoles' or similar, with boiled rice as the bulk and with canned meat or fish as flavourings. The rissoles were fried in any oil or fat one could obtain, the most usual being coconut oil or butter which had a strong and very characteristic smell, but sometimes we used red palm oil and only very rarely animal fat. The Australians called these rissoles 'doofers', the name being a contraction from 'hors d'oeuvres' (horse doofers). The quality and quantity of one's private cooking depended entirely upon what was available, sometimes stolen but mostly bought with money from stolen merchandise. Thus the quality of one's diet depended largely upon one's ability as a thief and smuggler.

If one had a whole can of bully beef, say, it could not be eaten by just one person. Once opened, such foods would not keep, and so sharing was essential. Douglas and I shared everything but even then, sometimes the quantity was such that we would need to offer some to our friends. Apart from the economy, it also made for variety, a feature which throughout my three and a half years as a prisoner was completely lacking except for the time in The Great World.

On 28th October 1942 we heard that our stay in The Great World was coming to an end, the popular rumour being that we were to go 'up country' to a rest camp. At that time the term was not a euphemism, and it was not until a long time later that stories filtered back to Singapore regarding the now infamous railway through Thailand. The first move came on 2nd November when we moved to a transit camp only a short distance away on the River Valley Road.

Until quite recently River Valley had been a working camp like ours but most of its occupants had already been sent north. As soon as possible, I went to inspect the theatre but, not having had the back-up facilities which we had been so fortunate to find in The Great World, it was a very primitive affair by comparison. With my mind full of uncertainties, I felt no urge to do anything about it and rather sadly left the stage. As I climbed down the rough step ladder my left foot landed on a long and rusty nail which was sticking up from the lowest step. With most of my weight on it, the nail went through the rubber sole of my plimsole and deep into my foot. With some difficulty I pulled myself free and immediately hobbled to the MO who cleaned the wound as best he could and painted it with iodine. Unfortunately but predictably, it soon began to hurt like hell and two days later my left foot was as big as a football. Both the MO, Australian Doctor Pete Hendry, and Captain Cole told me firmly that I could not go north with the party and must return to Changi next day. There was no denying the sense of that decision but I was saddened because it meant parting from Douglas and my other friends.

Early in the morning of Thursday, 7th November 1942 I was helped into a truck and with two or three other sick men was driven back to Changi.

The author in 1941

On the Nasik Road, India, June 1941

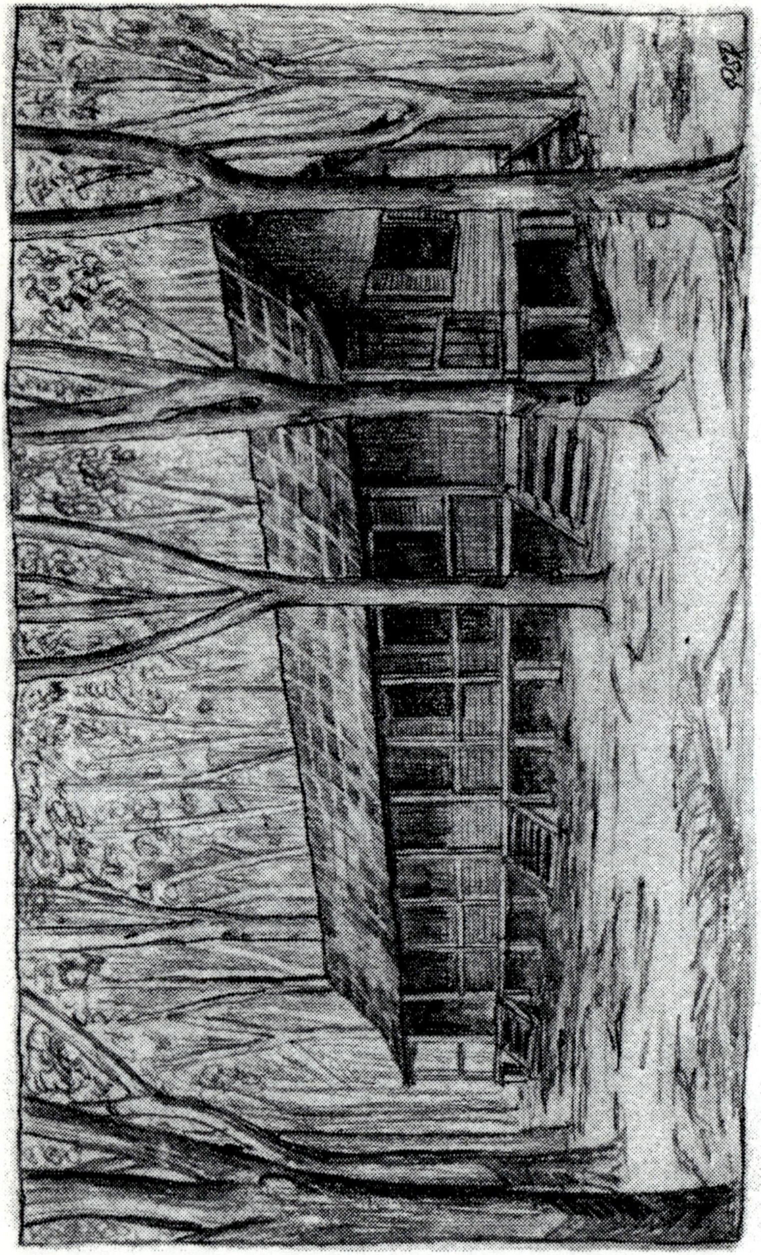

Billet in the Rubber Trees, Ipoh, Malaya, September 1941

Malay kampong near Sungai Patani, November 1941

Tongkangs at Chew Pier, Georgetown

Dr. Hen van Rappard, Mizumaki-cho, Kyushu, Japan, 1944

Pushing up the empty trucks, 1954 (a memory sketch)

Chuzo Maeda (The Pig), 1945

Part of the British Party, P.S.R. seated left on front row, 20th August 1945

The First Air Drop, 20th August 1945

CHAPTER SIX

BACK TO CHANGI

Some report of my theatrical activities in The Great World must have reached Changi before me. We had just driven through the gate when a sergeant on duty there gave me a note which asked that at my earliest convenience I should report to Major Cyril Avery, RIAOC, the Entertainments Officer. I limped back to the hut where I had lived with other members of the 155 before going to Singapore and there, happily, I found Tiger Robinson and a few other friends. Fortunately, there was an empty bed near Tiger and I flopped down on it, grunting with the pain of my foot. Someone gave me a mug of water and after I had rolled a cigarette we talked, exchanging all the news we had.

After a shower and a change of clothes my first call was to the MO who re-dressed my foot and gave me an injection of something. Then, after a drab but typical Changi lunch of reasonably well-cooked rice and some watery bully beef stew, I hobbled away to look for the Entertainments Officer. Major Cyril Avery, of the Royal Indian Army Ordnance Corps, was a kindly-looking man of about forty-five years of age. (I was then 23.) He was tall and looked very emaciated but I suspect that he had always been lean and fit. When I found him in his billet in the Ordnance lines he was puffing at an empty pipe, was naked to the waist and wore a pair of rope sandals which, I learned later, he had made himself. After inquiring at some length about my foot and my general health he said that he had indeed heard of my activities in The Great World and now hoped that I might be able to stage a pantomime for Christmas, which was just one month away?

The Major explained that the best players of a once very active concert party had gone 'up country', taking with them most of the costumes, make-up and so on. We walked a short distance to the theatre, a mono-pitch, atap-roofed and open-sided shelter for vehicles.

The stage was a small enclosure at one end, and the seating for about two hundred was long benches made from coconut palm trunks, sawn in half lengthwise. The stage lighting was from about six motor car headlamp bulbs powered by two or three car batteries. I was not impressed! Back in the Major's billet, we discussed the problem but with no good result, and I promised to think about it overnight.

I could not think of any good ideas that evening, and it was not until dawn that I had an idea. After various failed experiments, I made a blank lantern slide out of cellophane, the precursor of modern transparent plastic sheet, sandwiched between two cut-out cardboard frames. On the slide I painted a black line drawing of a seaside scene, complete with palm trees, then I took it to Major Avery. The idea was that if someone could write a script, and someone else could illustrate it, rather like a strip cartoon in the newspapers, I could copy the cartoons onto slides. Then unseen readers, not necessarily actors, could read the script from behind a screen while the slides would be projected onto the screen. I further explained that I still had the lenses from our survey instruments, and with these I was sure that a lantern could be made. I suggested calling the show a 'Phantomime'.

Major Avery was obviously intrigued and asked me to come back on the morrow, by which time he hoped to have had an idea. When the appointed time arrived, he handed me a paper on which was written some lines of verse, the introduction to a story, described as 'Crusoe - up-to-date'. Fascinated, I read on to discover that this was going to be a complete story in verse about a modern Robinson Crusoe. 'Who wrote this?', I asked. 'It's great!' 'Charles Arnold.' 'Oh? Who's he?' Major Avery smiled and pointed to himself. When pressed further, he revealed that over the years in India he had written several stories, all under the pen-name of Charles Arnold, and he preferred to use it rather than his own. From that moment on, by his smiling agreement, I always called him Charles and even now it is difficult to think of him by any other name. Charles went on to say that he had found a man to draw the cartoons: another RIAOC officer, Lt. Bob Simpson who, I was told later, was really a Russian. Bob and I discussed methods of production for the slides, and then had to wait a short time while Charles finished the script, which he did in only five days.

The story, all in verse but with metrical variations, took young Crusoe into marriage and then, after drinking too much with an old friend, into a drunken dream. In it he met an Ancient Mariner and set sail from the Surrey Docks in the brig 'Susanna' on a Friday, May 13th in the year 1698. The ship met a violent storm and was wrecked in about two degrees of north latitude and some hundred degrees east. (Bearings recognisable to most of us as the location of Singapore.) Cast ashore alone, Crusoe met a native whom he called Friday who revealed that:

The island wasn't desert! The hinterland was packed
With Friday's near relations. (He mentioned aunts and cousins.)
Interrogated re his wives, he simply murmured 'Dozens!'

Crusoe visited the tribe, met and courted Friday's sister, a very buxom lass called Sparewheela and was then caught and sentenced to death for flirting with an engaged woman. He and Friday were both in a large cookpot and being cooked for a feast when they managed to escape. After wandering around for many years, they met the General, a survivor from Changi POW camp who, having become so accustomed to the rules (his) when the war ended, did not want to go home and:

...was permitted to purchase his pen,
But found it most difficult, lacking the men,
To run things in a regular way, so when Crusoe and Friday turned up he felt gay.

The next half-hour poked fun at all the petty rules and regulations of Changi life, such as pulling the ration trailers, the always empty canteen, black marketers, Jap flags as passports, and the hoarding of canned foodstuffs. The sad tale ends with the finding of the General drinking in his own private liquor store. Crusoe and Friday pounced on the General, tied him up and then proceeded to slake a thirst they'd had for years, until 'Friday beneath the table slid. Then, one drink later, Crusoe did. Crusoe eventually awoke to find...', but I'll leave the end of the story for a short time.

My damaged left foot steadily improved as I got on with the making of the Robinson Crusoe slides, working for as long as possible during daylight, and in the evenings I joined the concert party as stage manager. The producer and originator of most of the items was Lt. K.G. Morison of the RIAOC, who had been a professional compère in Scarborough. We used all kinds of material and of course there was never any thought about copyright. Our regular pianist was Lieut. Geoff Knight of the 80th Anti-tank Regiment, RA, a good musician but also an excellent anchor man who never forgot or varied a cue.

A few days before Christmas, 1942, the Japanese issued an order to the effect that: 'All men will be happy.' To encourage that condition they would provide, as a gift from the Emperor to mark his great generosity, one tin of pineapple between six and one woman between twelve. The former was accepted but the latter was declined, with thanks, of course! At least that is the story as told at the time, and I saw no reason to disbelieve it.

Geoff Knight was an excellent concert party pianist as well as being a useful contributor of ideas for items in the shows. Greatly valued by all the performers and also by me as stage manager was his ability to remember the details of musical routines so that, once we had agreed upon a piece of music and its introduction, Geoff never varied it. This meant that in addition to providing the musical accompaniment he also acted as a sort of 'anchor man' on whom we all relied. When Christmas arrived, apparently Geoff and some friends got hold of some home made strong liquor and then went for a late evening stroll on the padang, a large open area of grass, originally a sports field. There were many prisoners strolling in the cool of the evening, self included, and suddenly Geoff decided that he wanted to 'address the troops'. He clambered up onto an empty oil drum and then urged us to: 'Look at the moon, the full moon, terang boolan (Malayan for Full Moon, now the National Anthem of Malaysia but then a saucy love song), and remember that your loved ones, your wives and sweethearts are looking at the same moon!' Then he staggered a little and would have fallen off his barrel, had I not rescued him and escorted him back to his billet. After all, he was our pianist and we needed him for the next night's show. Next day, and back with the making of the slides, I drew a joke advert about 'Glamourous Moonlight Knight' to commemorate the event.

During my first period in Changi, between March and May 1942, I had earned a little money or its equivalent by making things and so was able to buy a few extras for private cooking, as well as some tobacco and cheroots. But during the second period, between November 1942 and May 1943, I was too busy with theatre work. Unfortunately, unlike the Australian Concert Party which was kept apart and given special rations, there was no 'pay' of any kind for the 'Pow-Wows', the 11th Indian Division Concert Party, and so unless something drastic was done I was going to remain hungry. The upshot was that after one of the shows and at about one o'clock in the morning I joined three or four men from the 155 on a clandestine sortie to the nearest of the big coastal guns. The purpose of the raid was to look for diesel oil that we could then sell as an illuminant.

We equipped ourselves with big cans or buckets in which to bring back the oil, and we set out round the back of the padang, through the long grass on our stomachs, under the barbed wire boundary fence and on through more long grass to the gun. We had to be quiet because there were Sikh guards patrolling just outside the wire, and we had no idea what might be at the gun. The distance was not great; perhaps a hundred yards from the padang, but it took us a long time to get there. We were lucky to find that the wooden door to the concrete emplacement was unlocked. Inside, everything was deep below ground, in a shaft of about fifteen feet diameter. It was hard to see anything in the near complete darkness but one of my friends inched forward, found the edge of the pit, and by feeling round the rim, found the ladder.

The descent was difficult because we each had to carry our big containers in one hand, and silence was still thought to be necessary. One behind the other we climbed slowly down into the black pit of unknown depth, and although it was reasonable to assume that there were no Nips down there, nevertheless I must admit that I felt a real excitement. We paused on a landing while the leader felt around to find another ladder, then down we went again, and several minutes later we arrived at the bottom. Someone struck a match and lit a stump of candle and we then were able to see the large oil tank We began to fill our containers, and meanwhile someone found a coil of rope. That solved our problem of how to get the full and heavy containers back up to the top, although we still had to do it in two lifts, landing to landing. Finally we had to get those cans, mostly with wide-open tops, through the long grass, under the wire, round the edge of the padang and back to our hut. It took seemingly ages and I for one was aching all over long before we had finished. We all had sore elbows and knees.

At the billet, a hut like those in Ipoh and Sungai Patani but raised only about two feet above the ground, we emptied our oil into a petrol tank from a discarded truck, which was then buried under the hut and directly below my bed. It stayed there untouched for a couple of days until someone found a length of copper tubing and I acquired a mechanical petrol pump, which we fastened to the inside of my bed leg. From there we dispensed the oil in small quantities and for a very reasonable price, considering all our risk, sweat and stress, and when the proceeds were shared out we were all able to buy a modest amount of extras. We should have liked to make a second sortie but unfortunately, soon after our trip some Dutchmen went to the gun. Not content with taking oil, they also took tools - which the Japanese missed!

Although I did my best with the Crusoe slides: seventy-two for the show itself and another twelve for joke adverts at the beginning, and each coloured with photo tints from a book of colours contributed by someone, they were not ready in time for Christmas but we did open one week later, on 1st January 1943.

For the staging we had an eight-foot square screen and behind this was a large speaker cone which we had collected from the disused cinema in Changi village. The electric part of the speaker had been removed and in its place was a twin mouthpiece made by friends in Divisional Signals Workshop. The two mouthpieces were at the right height for speakers sitting on a bench and reading from copies of the script which were on a table below the speaker cone. It took some hard rehearsal to drill the readers to slide in and out of the reading positions at the correct times, and I marked up a copy of the script specially for that purpose. Charles, with the marked script, saw that it was followed exactly.

Behind the readers was a small string orchestra provided by some Dutchmen, and two singers stood in the wings, all to provide some musical relief.

When the time to begin arrived, Ken Morison and I walked out from each side of the stage, he to take his place as Narrator at a lectern on the audience's left and I to walk down the centre aisle to the projector. This had been made by Div. Sigs. Workshop to my design and using lenses from our survey instruments. The lamp was a car headlamp bulb, and halfway through the one-hour show I had to change the battery. The audience went quiet and one could then hear the never-ending sound of cicadas and other insects. On the breeze was a strong smell of hot coconut oil, from someone nearby doing a little private cooking, and someone else was smoking a cigarette which smelled like burning grass, which it probably was. The orchestra played 'Poor Old Robinson Crusoe'; the show was beginning.

As I was saying: 'First Friday 'neath the table slid.
Just one drink later, Crusoe did.
He woke to hear the awful knell
Of what he thought was Friday's bell,
Then realised with pleasing shock
It was his modern alarm clock.
And then he saw his Daphne stand,
A moistened sponge held in her hand,
Ready to wake him, should the hail
Of that, his usual rouser fail.
Then Daphne sat down on the bed, stopped the alarm clock, stroked his head
And said: "How is my naughty child? I'm sorry I last night was wild,
But I'd been waiting hours, you know, to tell you a great secret, so – "
And here she whispered in his ear.
Crusoe sat up and shouted: "Joy! Let's hope that it will be a boy!"
Wild horses now could not detain Crusoe from his usual train
And every night he'll homeward run to watch the bathing of his son.
When in the office juniors say
How much they wish to run away
He then relates the story true

Which we have just passed on to you;
And soon for us, come when it may,
We know that there must dawn a day
When Changi life and Changi fare
Will seem a distant, past nightmare.'

Every night when Ken Morison spoke the last line I felt a sort of tingle down my spine and, do you know, I have just felt the same tingle again as I typed the same magic words of hope.

The show at The Rice Bowl theatre for the second week in January 1943, following on after 'Robinson Crusoe', was 'The Admirable Dyeton'. This was a complete play lifted, without any thought of royalties, from J. M. Barrie's 'Admirable Crichton' and was produced by a group of officers from another unit. At that time, as stage manager, my only concern was to familiarise myself with the script and to stage the show. Most of the scenery was supposed to be a background of jungle and so a large quantity of real greenery was stacked on the stage. A personal contribution was to make with my mouth and hands the hooting sound of the steamship which eventually arrived, unseen, to take home all the characters in the play.

All went well for the first three nights but on the fourth, Thursday, only a few minutes before the sound of the siren was due, I felt something large moving in the front of my shirt just above my belt. And then I was stung, first on the left and then on the right of my stomach. I tugged out my shirt but in the darkness I could see nothing. Within moments my waistline was in considerable pain but I hung on long enough to make the sound of the hooter. Then, after a quick word to one of the players, I dashed from the stage to the nearest medical hut, about two hundred yards away. In considerable distress, I received from a kindly Indian doctor two shots of cocaine, and then an Indian soldier escorted me back to my billet.

I don't remember much about the next twenty-four hours but Tiger Rob told me that I was thrashing and ranting for most of that time. For the next two or three weeks I had quite bad pain in both sides of my waist, and the marks of the bites were visible for the next twenty years or so. I suppose it was a centipede; I never actually saw it!

Several weeks passed after our expedition to the big gun. The later raid by the Dutchmen had alerted the Nips but nothing happened in my area, and it would have been about mid-January 1943 when those thoughtless, and selfish, Dutchmen again went to the gun, and again took tools. The Nips made a full search of Birdwood camp and while I was working in the theatre, still nursing a rather painful waistline, they found the petrol tank and the pump tied to my bed leg. I was arrested by two Nips who were waiting until I returned from the theatre for the evening meal, and I was frog-marched to the eiso or lock-up near the gate. There I was prodded with a rifle and accused: 'You tief!' There was nothing to say so I remained silent and received a good bashing of the usual full arm swing type. Then I was pushed roughly into the small, windowless and very smelly cubicle, little larger than the average WC, which was the lock-up, and was left there all night. There was nothing at all in that cubicle and so I had perforce to sleep on the slatted wooden floor which, by the stench, had also served as a urinal. Anxiety and uncertainty combined to ensure that it was not a good night.

Next morning two guards dragged me out and in front of their sergeant, who said only the same two words as before: 'You tief!' I wondered who had stolen what from whom, but I was in no mood or condition to express any such thoughts. The sergeant motioned to the two men, one of whom gave me a spade, and I was pushed by two rifles, out of the guardroom and across the north side of the padang. In the far corner the guards indicated that I should dig a trench of about six feet long, and in the hot sun and with the ground full of granite stones and gravel, that was very hard work.

After some time, I should guess about three quarters of an hour, the Nip sergeant arrived and I was ordered to stand to attention at the foot of the grave I had just dug, while the two guards retired about six paces and took aim.

My thoughts, such as they are remembered, were of the occasion when Douglas and I had first lain in the mosquito drain during the air raid. I was quite sure that death was only minutes away and I just went numb, quite resigned to my fate.

We all stood like that, motionless and silent, for what seemed like ages until the sergeant muttered something. The aimed rifles were lowered, and he had me by the ear, pushing and dragging me back towards the guardroom. Halfway there he let go of my ear and the two soldiers took over with the points of their rifles. Then I was pushed back into the cell and left alone for hours. I had no idea of the time, being quite in the dark, but at one time, perhaps midday, the door was unlocked and a cupful of water was pushed in.

I had not had any food since the usual midday meal of the day before, but the pangs of hunger had passed long ago, scarcely noticed because of the discomfort and a general state of anxiety. It was dreadfully hot in that cell but I managed to doze, if not really to sleep, most of the time sitting in a corner with my knees drawn up. I could hear voices from somewhere in the wooden building, presumably the Nips in the guardroom, but nobody came near me for several hours.

Then, with surprisingly little shouting, the two soldiers had me out again and blinking in the evening sunlight. I was given the spade again, marched back to the far side of the padang, and told to deepen the grave I had dug yesterday. Then, as before, the sergeant arrived and once again I had to stand to attention and face the two rifles pointed at me.

Next morning the performance was repeated, and again I had to face those two rifles, expecting to be shot. As before, nothing happened and I was marched back to the eiso. Once inside the guardroom, the sergeant removed my spectacles and then proceeded to give me a long and hard bashing around the head, such that my ears were ringing and it took all my will power and small remaining strength to remain standing. I had seen before that a man who failed to stand got kicked in the ribs. Eventually the bashing stopped, presumably because the sergeant was becoming tired. My specs were stuck back on my face and I was pushed out of the guardroom, to fall to my knees on the ground outside. I was too dizzy to get up immediately but after a short time the two soldiers came out and hauled me to my feet, pointed me in the direction of my billet and gave me a push with their rifles. I staggered back to my hut and collapsed on my bed. Somebody gave me a lighted cigarette and someone else offered me a cup of water. By midday I felt a lot better and went to collect my own lunch of some slightly soggy rice and some very watery bully stew. That evening I was back in the theatre.

Strangely enough, the Nips made no move to confiscate the tank and the remaining oil, which lasted for several months more. I never heard of any other trips to the big gun, although expeditions through the wire continued.

We did two more shows in the Rice Bowl theatre after 'The Admirable Dyeton' and then, about the end of January 1943, we moved our business to a new building nearer to Changi Village. The move came when the 11th Indian Division in Birdwood Camp combined with Southern Command Area and moved to their theatre. It had been built before the war as an open-air concert stage and its auditorium was a large semi-circular dell wherein the audience just sat on the grassy slopes. It was a vast improvement for us, with a quite large stage, a good curtain, some limited facility for flying scenery, and electric light with a good supply of high-wattage lamps. There was also an orchestra pit. Now, we felt, we could really work to put on some good shows, and we did just that.

Southern Area, like Indian Division, had lost a lot of players to parties going 'up-country' but there were two or three good men left who were happy to be in a good concert party once more. Also, they still had several very competent musicians so that instead of having Geoff Knight alone at his piano we suddenly had a full pit orchestra, with Geoff still at the piano and giving the intro-cues as before. In the orchestra was Tommy Carlisle who had been the Number Two in the accordion band on the Strathmore. Amongst our new friends was a Russian, whose name I forget, who acted as the conductor but who was also able to orchestrate and write out the parts for any tune required. The total effect was wholly professional and greatly appreciated, both by the Concert Party and by our audience.

As before, we played every night of the week except Sundays when, in the afternoons, we took suitable excerpts on tour to the hospitals. The nights of the week were allocated to the different Units so that, for instance, the 155 always came on a Wednesday, and the Australians always came on a Friday.

Although in the New Rice Bowl Theatre we had plenty of electric light, we still did not have any colour - until I spent more time in thought and came up with an idea, after which we had plenty of brilliantly coloured light, and became the envy of the other theatre stage-managers. On two or three occasions visitors would come to the stage door after the show and ask to see the stage and they were always told: 'Yes, by all means. But just wait a minute, please'. It took only a minute to tidy up and then, as they came onto the stage they would look around and up to some bare lamps above, and finally would ask: 'But where's your coloured light?' And do you know, I never would tell!

The explanation was polarised light, using big pieces of flat windscreen glass from discarded trucks as polariser and analyser, and large sheets of cellophane from big packets of cheap cheroots, laid between sheets of window glass and rotated as a means of providing the variable interference. After a little experimentation I was able, at will, to produce beautiful and vivid colours, the only snags being that we lost about two thirds of the illumination, and that the equipment was rather large. The idea was remembered from a little toy gadget I had made while still at school, but in The Rice Bowl there were six of those gadgets and each was as big as a dustbin. When not in use they were kept in a screened off bay at the side of the stage but even if seen, there was no colour and no reason for it unless one understood the secret. The big light boxes were beautifully made out of assorted scrap wood to my design by the stage carpenter, Capt. Bill Davies, RIAOC. In the Great World I had done all my own carpentry but in Changi Bill made everything and did a great job.

For the next three and a half months I did nothing but concert party work. I still slept beside Tiger and drew my food from the 155's cookhouse but immediately after breakfast, I went to the theatre and spent the morning with Bill Davies and Peter Pierce, who was a corporal in the Royal Corps of Signals but now was the stage electrician. We made, painted and wired up all the sets and props for the next week's show. In the afternoon Bill was left to get on with the carpentry while Peter and I joined Ken Morison, Geoff Knight and an assortment of players on the stage to rehearse for next week's show.

There was then a pause for the evening meal and about an hour of rest before we all returned to play the current show, after which all the players went back to their billets, although three or four of us would then retire to Ken Morison's billet to write the show for the week after next. Sometimes we were joined by Col. E C O Morphy, RIAOC, who came up with some good ideas for items and also for songs, both words and music. Once or twice he took a playing part, under the name of 'Eric Owen', and was known to all the party as Eric, After the war he was invited, in the rank of Major General, to set up an Ordnance Corps for the newly independent India. After retirement he wrote several newspaper articles about POW days.

Thanks to the almost continuous demand of the theatre, the ever-present hunger did not dominate me quite as much as it did for so many other men. However, life in Changi was steadily becoming worse. Several drafts were taken away to work somewhere in the north, but we never knew any details of their destination or of the work involved. My name appeared on successive drafts but was later removed so that I could continue as stage manager. I never knew who did the removal and I thought it prudent never to ask.

Tiger Robinson and I were the last two surveyors of the 155 in Changi and he, poor chap, was having trouble with a complaint called: 'Happy Feet'. Caused by vitamin B deficiency, this was a spasmodic sensation of burning and pricking of the feet, particularly the soles. I had it only slightly but Tiger was much troubled, both day and night. He kept two large buckets of water beside his bed and at any time, day or night, would plunge his feet and keep them there until the cold water had put out the fire.

I had trouble with tropical ulcers and although they remained comparatively small, they were all over my legs and becoming worse, so that something had to be done, Then I heard that the next draft was to Japan and, purely as a means of getting out of the tropics, I let it be known that I wished to go. Thus my name stayed on the list and the die was cast. The Pow Wows gave me a 24-bass piano accordion to take with me, and a few of us had a modest farewell party.

CHAPTER SEVEN

PRISONER OF WAR IN JAPAN

On Sunday, 16th May 1943, about nine hundred other men and myself, most of them strangers to me, were crammed into a small cargo ship of less than 4,000 tons. I never heard its name but was told that a plate on the bridge stated that it was originally registered in Cardiff. Someone called it the Mukki Maru and the name stuck. Presumably it had been sold to the Japanese for scrap some years earlier, and that was just what the leaky old tub was fit for. The lower parts of the holds were filled with some unknown cargo and we were stowed with maximum density in the upper parts. We had about nine square feet of floor space per man; not enough to allow one to lie down without sticking ones feet into someone else.

Where the floor extended to the sides of the ship and beyond the limits of the cargo hatch, a distance of about eight feet, the total height of about ten feet was divided by an inserted gallery or shelf of rough planks, thus doubling the sleeping space at the sides. However, the total available headroom in those areas was at most four and a half feet. I found myself allotted an unmarked spot roughly in the middle of the forward or No.1 hold, which I shared with approximately 250 men.

Because I had been removed from so many of the earlier drafts there were few of the 155 with me and I had to become acquainted with many new comrades in adversity. Also, when units had nominated men for drafts, the fittest were always picked first, with the result that ours, a comparatively late one, consisted largely of sick men and with a few petty criminals who had missed the earlier drafts because they were 'in punishment'.

Somehow general cleanliness was maintained, although sometimes a man simply could not reach the latrines in time. These were up on deck and constructed of rough timber to cantilever over the side of the ship. No paper of any sort was available.

There were no washing facilities but once a day we were allowed up on deck to be hosed down with seawater. If one wanted to launder one's vest and shorts they were worn for the hosing; otherwise we went on deck completely naked. However, although it was certainly a 'hell ship', it did not smell anything like as badly as the SS Ekma which had carried the 155 from Bombay to Port Swettenham

We had two meals a day, consisting of a small amount of plain boiled rice and some watery vegetable soup. This was made partly with seawater and also with some shoyu or soya sauce. Although it was not very nourishing, in fact it had quite a good flavour - or so I thought at the time!

When we left Singapore our ship was one of six in a small convoy, and our first stop was at dawn on Wednesday, 19th May, when we anchored off Saigon. For most of that day we were kept below except for grudgingly allowed visits to the latrines. Then, just after sunset we heard the anchor being raised and the engines started up, after which, in the dark, we were allowed up on deck. There was just enough light left for me to count that we were now in a convoy of nine, with no vessel larger than ours.

After another ten days of slow progress on a zigzag course across the South China Sea, at mid-morning on Saturday, 29th May we arrived at Tainan, Formosa (now called Taiwan) and, with a few trips to the lats, I was able to see something of the scene. The entrance to the harbour was by a narrow, cliff-sided passage but, once through that, the habour widened out. In it there were many small ships, two appearing to be hospital ships. We stayed there in Tainan harbour without any event until Monday, 31st May when, just before dawn, we moved slowly through the narrow entrance and out into the bay, but there we stopped until about noon when we returned to the harbour. Our journey continued at dawn next day, Tuesday, 1st June. I had expected to turn to the right and head northward up the Formosa Strait but instead we turned left and southward round the southern tip of Formosa. Then, just out of sight of land, we turned north and into the East China Sea.

Every day until now the weather had been calm and clear and, of course, tropically hot, but on Wednesday, 2nd June we had a typhoon (from the Japanese: *tai fu*, a great wind). The sky was dark and we saw twisters or water spouts in the distance to the east. Gale force winds tipped the ship over to one side and movement on deck was difficult, particularly when going to or actually in the latrines, but yet, to my surprise, the surface of the sea remained remarkably unruffled. I think that was because the wind blew very steadily and without any noticeable gusting or veering. It was about this time that I remembered our long sea journey from Gouroch to Cape Town and on to Bombay. Then, for the first two or three days, large numbers of the company were seasick, but now, with a similar cross section of British soldiery, so far as I could see, not a single man was seasick. On that 'hell ship' we had other things on our minds.

The typhoon subsided in mid-afternoon and things returned to the normal uncomfortable monotony, but next day, Thursday, 3rd June, we had quite an event. We had had our morning meal and I was one of about twenty allowed up on deck for a breather. I was looking forward when suddenly I saw on our starboard bow a white streak moving rapidly towards us in the water. Those on the bridge saw it too and immediately the siren sounded. The Nip soldier guards immediately shouted and screamed, bundling us all down into the hold, but not before I saw the torpedo, presumed to be American, miss our bows by some thirty or forty feet. Then I was hit in the back with a rifle butt and fell the ten feet down into the hold. I landed on other men and was thus saved from damage other than a badly wrenched left ankle. Others, including some of those on which I landed, fared much worse.

The guards hastily covered up our hatch, leaving us helpless in the dark, and almost immediately we heard and felt the thuds of many depth charges. The noise continued for about a quarter of an hour, water began to spurt through joints in the plates, and the engine stopped. I heard later that it had suffered some damage but none of us knew much about it. We were kept battened down in that inky black hold for more than two hours, with the ship rolling around in very uncertain fashion, silent except for the splashing of water and the creaking and groaning sounds made by the damaged plates. When once again allowed up on deck, I saw that the other eight ships had gone, leaving us to limp our way alone across the East China Sea.

Four days later, we turned into the Inland Sea and at noon tied up at Moji, now part of Kitakyushu and on the south side of the Straits of Shimonoseki. We were two days late and this had meant that our rations during those last four days were cut to about half.

Many men became ill during the voyage and two men in No.1 hold died. Their bodies were taken up on deck but, as none of the prisoners was allowed up, I do not know how the Nips disposed of the bodies. I can only suppose that they were thrown overboard without ceremony. So far as I know, no attempt was made to record names; still less to pass the record to relatives.

Soon after berthing at Moji all nine hundred prisoners were rushed ashore and assembled on a patch of bare ground near the quay and facing the water. In front of us was a high timber rostrum with a ladder up the front. On the rostrum and to its rear were a table and some packing cases. After a wait of about half an hour a Japanese officer, complete with clanking sword, climbed up onto the rostrum and addressed the company in tolerably good English. We were now the guests of Great Japan, he said, and we must behave as befits a guest. We would be given shelter, food and clothing, but for these we must work. If we did not obey our new masters we would be punished, but if we behaved ourselves and worked well, he was confident that all men would be happy! (At that point I recalled the Christmas message from the IJA in Singapore.) And now, he continued, as we came into our new home it would never do if we brought disease with us. Therefore, every man must be tested. Officers first, please.

He then climbed down from the rostrum, his place being taken by a man in a white coat, while two young nurses took glass rods and culture dishes out of the packing cases. There was a short pause and then all our officers were hustled to the front and made to climb the ladder, one at a time. On the rostrum they each had to drop their trousers and bend over, with their bare backsides towards the company and a small group of local onlookers at the rear, whereupon one of the nurses inserted a glass rod and then wiped it onto one of the culture dishes. After all the officers had been so treated it was the turn of the men, the only difference being that we faced the crowd. When my turn came I looked closely at the procedure and at the pile of rods and dishes and noted that neither was for exclusive use. It was immediately apparent to me that the whole business was a charade intended to give an impression of scientific care, but also, and more importantly, to ridicule our officers in front of their men. The men did not laugh.

After the ceremony of the glass rod, the party was broken up into smaller groups and I found myself with about 200, none of whom I knew. I discovered later that in fact there were two groups: 94 British and 94 Australian; and two officers: an English subaltern and a South African captain doctor.

At about 4 p.m. we were marched a short distance to a railway siding and told to sit down and wait. There were armed guards all around us and after about half an hour more soldiers came and searched our tatty belongings, but they did not confiscate anything. By that time we all were very hungry, having had nothing since our half-ration breakfast on the ship. Another hour or so passed and then, escorted by more soldiers, some women wearing zubon or baggy trousers, and dark blue smocks came with big cans and we each received a tennis-ball-sized snowy white rice cake, doughy and slightly sweet, and a small ration of water. At about 7 p.m. we were marched in the dark a short distance and put aboard a train.

That train was quite a surprise. Until then everything we had seen in Japan had been cheap and shoddy but those coaches were of surprisingly good quality. The seats were in pairs, back-to-back, with a central aisle, the cream upholstery was clean and there was no graffiti on the cream paintwork. When we set off, the motion was smooth and very comfortable. As it was dark we could not see the engine, and in fact I never saw one until after the war. The terrain seemed to be largely urban, with buildings close by the line, and for the whole journey of about an hour there was a frequent clanging of bells as we passed many level crossings. I guessed that the distance would have been between 30 and 40 miles, although I could not be certain. Eventually, at between 8.00 and 9.00 p.m., the train stopped and we were hustled out. I learned later that the name of the station was Orio.

Carrying all our belongings, we trudged for two hours or more in the darkness along rutted and muddy tracks, often between high hedges, and accompanied by the sound of many insects. Everyone was tired and many were really sick. My left ankle, damaged when the submarine attacked us, was still very painful but I managed to keep going, although many men stumbled and fell, to be kicked to their feet by the guards. I gathered later that some who fell were not brought in until several hours after the rest of us. When we were almost completely exhausted, we passed by some industrial structures, and there was a loud throbbing noise coming from some heavy compressors or similar machinery. The roadway became broader and then, about a quarter of a mile further on, we turned to the right, crossed some railway tracks and staggered in through a big gate in a high wooden fence. We had arrived at our new camp and the time was about 11.30 p.m.

It was not until after the war had ended, that I discovered that from our camp to Orio station, along good roads, was less than a fifteen-minute walk. It then became clear that our long trudge in the dark had had but one purpose: to disorientate us.

Soon the new arrivals were divided into two groups: British and Australian, and led to two barrack blocks in the south east corner of the camp. Those barrack blocks, of which there were twelve, were really terraces of ten houses each, built by the mining company to hold civilian workers and their families. I later learned that the company was the Nittan Takamatsu Tanko Kaisha, and that there were similar civilian estates in the neighbourhood

Constructed almost entirely of unpainted wood and roofed with dark grey pantiles, each had two rooms, one above the other, all linked on the western side by a covered corridor, and on the eastern side at first floor by a gallery which, we were told, was reserved for the guards. The floors were of rice straw mats, 6 feet by 3 feet, and 2 inches thick, covered with a light fawn coloured mat of fine woven grass-like material called igusa. The mats themselves, the traditional floor covering in Japan, were called *tatami*. There were four *tatam*i in each of the lower rooms and six in the upper ones, and we had one mat per man. I was put into the lower room of House No. 4 in Block No. 11. Our two officers were given the end upstairs rooms in the two blocks; Lt. Derek Humber was in Block 11 with the British, while Captain Nairnsey was in the similar room in Block 12, with the Australians.

Entrance to the blocks was by a sliding door at each end of the covered corridor, inside which was a concrete walkway and beyond this a wooden step, some two and a half feet wide and about a foot high.

As we entered the barrack block our first instruction was to remove our boots on the concrete and never to walk on the wooden walkway or tatami in other than bare or stockinged feet. This was a new concept for us but the need for the rule was immediately apparent. Access to the upper room was by a steep and narrow wooden stair leading directly off the wooden step. The ground floor room was separated from the step by a pair of sliding screens, called shoji, consisting of light frames of pine laths over which was pasted thin but strong paper.

On each *tatami* we found two small but thick cotton blankets, a very short-sleeved jacket and a pair of shorts, both made of a rough hessian-like material, a cotton loincloth, some shapeless cotton socks, a pair of rubberised canvas boots with a cleft big toe, a pair of short puttees, a pillbox-shaped cap of American cloth, and a rubberised canvas belt. There was also a galvanised metal water bottle, a lacquered wooden lunch box and a small square of purple rayon in which to wrap it, and a small cotton sweat towel.

Minutes later, we were hustled out, across a central parade ground and to a large building, the shokudo (dining room) where we found wooden trestle tables already set with two bowls per man. One was generously full of plain boiled rice, on the top of which was a small dried and salted fish, while the other contained a watery vegetable soup. A Dutch officer, Captain de Vries, introduced himself and welcomed us to the camp. He warned us that we should do our best to eat all that was set before us because if we did not do so the Japanese would merely reduce the ration. How right he was! Unfortunately, while I and a few more managed very well, the majority were so sick or so tired that they could not have eaten much of anything, no matter how appetising it might have been.

Then Captain de Vries said that on all occasions before eating we must say a grace of one word: *Itadakimasu* (I partake). He made us rehearse it several times then invited us to eat, adding his own encouragement in Dutch: '*Smaaklijk eten, mijnheren!*' (Tasty eating, gentlemen!). Incidentally, although the word '*Itadakimasu*' is used generally in Japan, that was the only time we used it as a grace.

Half an hour later, a Japanese officer came in and was introduced by Captain de Vries as the Camp Commandant, but his name was not given. Aged about forty-five and slightly stout, he was immaculately dressed, complete with sword. He repeated some of the words we had heard at Moji and then revealed our future. We were to be coal miners. If we continued to work well we should be given food and good care, but if we did not work well we would be punished, and anyone trying to escape would be shot!

Captain de Vries then told us that we must always salute every Japanese soldier, irrespective of rank, and we should now stand and salute the Commandant. In doing so we must shout the word: *Keirei!* (Salute!). He rehearsed us twice and then invited the Commandant to take the salute, which he did before departing. After our meal de Vries introduced another Japanese word: *Itadakimashita* (I have partaken). We returned to our rooms at 1 a.m. and were soon asleep on our mats, too tired to do anything else.

Next morning at 6 a.m., after less than five hours sleep, we were woken by soldiers who signed that we must be in the mess room in half an hour and wearing our issued clothing. There was much comment when the jacket and shorts were donned, because they all appeared to be far too small. The boots had a cleft big toe, but it was not until a few days later that many of us had troubles with blisters, caused by rubbing in unaccustomed places.

At 7.30 a.m. we were assembled on the parade ground for tenko (roll call), along with a number of other men who, we discovered, were from the Dutch Army.

The Dutchmen were soon counted and dismissed but we, the newcomers, were kept back to be given a first lesson on how to count ourselves in Japanese. After this rather lengthy exercise we each were given a little wooden tablet with a small hole drilled near each end. On it was painted in black ink the three Japanese numerals representing our new prison number. I then became *yon hyaku hachi ju*, translated as '480'. We were told to tie the tablet onto our newly issued working jacket, and were advised to memorise the number and be prepared to answer to it at all times. Before the parade was dismissed another Dutch officer: Lt. Sliew de Chauvigny, called *Ichi ban* (Number One) by the Japanese, told us that we were to spend the next two days in camp before starting our training as miners.

Back in our rooms, the message came that we were to hand in all knives and all other gear except clothes, toiletries and books, and these were to be put in store. I surrendered my small piano accordion, my table knife and sundry pieces of carved perspex, the remnants of a part-time hobby in Changi. I was very reluctant to part with my sketches and the original script and slides of Robinson Crusoe, so I wrapped them in a piece of torn groundsheet and hid them below the *tatami* and supporting floorboards of my room.

We were also told that during those two days in camp every man must go to the barber, a Dutchman, to have our hair clippered to the scalp. As soap was an exceedingly rare commodity, it was generally accepted that this was not a bad idea, but there was much merriment when we first saw each other, and ourselves if we could find a mirror. Even the officers had to have a close clip, and those with moustaches were ordered to remove them. Our lieutenant wore a neat one and its retention was eventually but grudgingly permitted.

I then set out to explore the camp and, being interested in the buildings and their construction, I made some rough sketches in a small note book and on some scraps of paper which I had retained. There were no toilet facilities in the houses.

Each block had a separate latrine structure at its northern end, and outside this was a cold water tap and a concrete slab for laundry. Washing of the person was done in a communal bath house.

The Japanese method of bathing was and still is to undress in an anteroom and then to squat or stand at the side of a very large bath, taking a small wooden boxful of hot water from the bath, and with that to wash all over with soap. Other boxes of water are used to sluice away all the dirt and soap, the water splashing onto the tiled or concrete floor and running away down drain holes. Then, when completely clean, one climbs down into the large communal bath to sit on a submerged ledge around the sides of the bath, and to soak and relax in the very hot water.

I have done this many times in recent years and find it a most delightful social occasion, and very relaxing. In camp, however, because of the shortage of soap and of the all too numerous skin diseases from which we suffered, we were not permitted to get into the bath and had to be satisfied with washing on the side.

When we first came into the camp there was a plenty of nine-inch square wooden boxes but, as time passed, the nails rusted and the boxes fell apart, and no attempt was made to repair them. The usual recourse was to one's mess tin, but this was small and necessitated too many refills, always difficult when one was fighting for space in a bath house crammed with men coming 'off shift' from the mine. Usually the bath water was well heated by a wood and coal-burning furnace but sometimes, because of fuel shortages, the water was cold. This did not matter too much on warm summer days, but it did in the wintertime. It is perhaps only fair to record that the British and Australian party were at all times most punctilious about washing, but this did not always apply to the Dutchmen.

There were about 760 Dutch, including four officers, 95 British including one officer, 95 Australians including one officer (the South African doctor), and about 60 Americans with no officers. The whole complement was, I think, originally 1,000 prisoners, although many died during the two and a half years of our being in the camp. The four Dutch officers were very good at their job, being unafraid when standing up to the Japanese and in looking after their men. One of the Dutch officers was the camp doctor: Captain Henk van Rappard, and I shall have more to say about him later. He and I became quite friendly and he gave another prisoner, James Warner, and me lessons in speaking Dutch. I mention him now in relation to bathing habits. Knowing of my interest in architecture, he was urging Jim and me to go to the Netherlands after the war, to see the towns and the buildings, and I can still hear his voice: 'You know, Rhodes, the Dutchman is not always very clean about his body, but his streets are bea-u-tiful!' I have seen and agree on both points.

The washing of clothes was difficult because of the scarcity of soap and a complete lack of warm water. Lice were all too numerous and it was difficult to get rid of them. If one sat in the mess room next to someone who did not wash himself and his clothes with the greatest of care one was likely to be invaded. I have seen the little brutes crawling along the bench from one man to his neighbour.

Bed bugs were another matter. These made their homes in the tatami and in any small cracks in the walls of the room. When we first went into the camp, our rooms in Blocks 11 and 12 were free of the smelly little beasts but, as the years passed, we were moved around and had to live in houses previously occupied by men who were not so clean.

On Thursday, 10th June 1943 we began a ten-day period of training, with a so-called rest day on the Sunday. Some of our party were already sick and in the camp hospital block but, after *tenko*, the rest of us were marched out of the camp and to an open space near the mine head.

There we were introduced to about six elderly civilians who were to be our instructors. We were to call them *sensei*, teacher. They were all dressed alike with shirts of a greyish cotton material, and with baggy trousers ending just below the knee and tucked in to white or greyish puttees. Some had cotton jackets, and all those garments showed signs of much darning but were remarkably clean, although the lack of soap probably accounted for the general grey colour. They wore rubberised boots like ours, and they also had caps like ours. I learned later that this nondescript garb, based upon the soldier's dress, was called *koku min fuku* (national dress), an invention of the ruling warlords.

I also noticed that their manner of walking, and indeed that of most male Japanese at that time, was rather peculiar. Instead of swinging the foot forward only a small distance above the ground, they always seemed to lift the foot by at least an inch, and maybe two, so as to give the appearance of stamping. Nowadays, young Japanese do not walk like that, but one can still see older men, particularly in country districts, who have that same peculiar gait, probably learned when they were soldiers.

The first two days of training went well enough because we were being taught basic Japanese military commands, which were quite similar to our own, so that we had no difficulty in understanding what was wanted. However, at the order: '*Sai keirei!*' we had to salute by bowing deeply from the hips and with chin tucked in and hounds down the side seams of the trousers. We were also rehearsed many times at counting ourselves in Japanese while standing in line. At the shouted command: *Bango!* (Number) we would sound off: *Ichi, ni, san, shi, go,* etc. and it took some time to grasp that the number 4 is sometimes *shi* (which also means death) and sometimes *yon*, and that 7 is sometimes *shichi* and sometimes *nana*. One or two of the men, either from birth or as the result of their privations, were very slow on the uptake, but most of us learned that much of the language fairly easily.

Later, however, when we moved on to learn something about our future work as coal miners, we struck trouble almost immediately. This, as we had found in Singapore, was entirely as the result of difficulty of communication, and our elderly teachers were soon exasperated. We had learned long ago that there was no profit in acting dumb and so were genuinely doing our best. But still the message did not get through, and the *sensei* were just about to use their sticks on us.

It was then that one of our number, a small and bespectacled man, stepped forward and bowed. Then he said some words in Japanese:'*Gomen nasai. Watashitachi wa Nihon-go wo wakarimasen*.' (Excuse me. We do not understand Japanese). There was a sudden hush and then our teachers muttered amongst themselves for a while. Eventually, they turned to us again and, much to our surprise, they almost smiled as, with considerably more patience, they tried again to explain and pass on their message.

We were grateful to our colleague whose name, I learned a little later, was Tommy Cowin. It was several days later when I heard the story about the kitten down the borehole in Changi. When we returned to camp that evening the leader of the sensei reported to the guardroom and a minute later he reappeared and pointed out Cowin to one of the soldiers. Tommy was taken into the guardroom - and that was the last we saw of him for five or six days. Rumours were plentiful but we gathered that Tommy was in the eiso (lock-up), accused of being a spy. This arose, apparently, solely because he spoke a few words of Japanese and that, for reasons not understood at the time, worried the *kempei tai* (Japanese secret police). When Tommy was released, on Monday 21st June, a rest day, we learned that he had been knocked about a bit, and had been given only a small amount of water during his confinement. Tommy's treatment by the *kempei tai* was an early indication that it would be wise to conceal any linguistic ability, however limited.

During the remainder of the training period we were introduced to an assortment of tools which we would have to use. These included a *jakama*; no trouble with that. It was a jack-hammer or rock drill. Then came a *piku* which was a pneumatic pick, with a removable bit called a nomi (chisel), but when an odd looking long-handled pickaxe was produced and called a *tsurubashi* there was a hold up as we tried to pronounce the strange name. Then a joker at the back called it a shitorbust and the name stuck among the English speaking prisoners for the next two and a half years. The tools most used by us in the days to come, apart from the jack-hammer, were the *ebu* and *kake-ita*. The *ebu*, called a *kago* elsewhere than in *Kyushu*, was an open fronted basket made of split and woven bamboo, while the *kake-ita* (from *kaku* - to scrape, and *ita*, a board) was a large draw-hoe with a steel blade and a wooden handle about eighteen inches long. We were shown how to use the *kake-ita* to scrape coal from a heap into the *ebu* held between the ankles, and then we had to practise with it. That work, involving bending over and staying like that for a long time while scraping, was very tiring and someone asked for a shovel, trying to explain that for us it would be much quicker and easier, but we were quickly told: '*shaberu nai*!' (there are no shovels). It was not until nearly two years later that I actually saw and handled one.

After nine days of work training we had another rest day, largely spent in doing camp fatigues, and then on Tuesday 22nd June 1943 we began our work underground. After an early breakfast of plain boiled rice and a bowl of watery vegetable soup we had our *bento baku* (picnic lunch boxes) three quarters filled with the same rice and four thin slices of salt-pickled daikon, a vegetable like a parsnip but bitter like a radish. After *tenko* the Dutchmen were marched out, and we soon followed. We turned left and at the mine head, about a quarter mile away, we were divided into sections of about twelve men each, called *buntai.* Each section was in the charge of a Japanese coal miner called *buntai cho* (section leader). I was put into *Nana buntai* (No. 7 Section) with a brawny, bad-tempered looking man as *buntai cho*. Then, section by section, we were led into the lamp house and each received a lamp and battery. The lamp was lit and there was no switch. We were shown how to thread the battery onto our belt and to wear it at the back, and the lamp was then clipped onto a fibre bracket at the front of the cap. The battery was very heavy and for the first ten days or so most of us had bruised stomach muscles, caused by the unaccustomed pressure of the belt. Again there was a brief pause because of language difficulties. The cap was called boshi but the lamp was called *capu*, the explanation being that the Japanese names were copied from the English but then shortened. Thus a cap-lamp, expressed in Japanese as *capu rampu*, was shortened to *capu*.

When we had been searched for cigarettes and matches, the whole company was arrayed on the flat ground outside the lamp house, called to attention and made to turn half left to face a rocky hill across the road. We were then told that the kami sama (spirit of the mine) lived in the hill and we must bow politely to it before entering the mine, and again when we came out. There was some quiet muttering amongst the men but we had learned long ago that any action smacking of mockery or derision would attract an immediate beating. Nevertheless, some men were thought not to be bowing deeply enough and were immediately pounced on and battered into an approved attitude of submission and supplication. We were also told that whenever we met someone else down the mine we should greet each other with the words: '*O anzen ite*' (Go in safety).

Eventually we were led by our *buntai cho*, through the double doors of an air lock, and into the dimly lit top station of the rope-hauled railway that was to take us down into the pit. Charlie Warnes, one of our number who was older than most and so called Pop, had been a miner before the war and he immediately remarked: 'That's the smell of the pit!'. For me the dank odour was a vivid reminder of some of the stations on the Mersey Underground Railway

The twin sets of narrow gauge track sloped down to the south-east. The tunnel had a slope of between 25 and 30 degrees, presumably following the dip of the geological strata. At its mouth the haulage cables passed over rollers so that the track in the station was at a slightly less slope. There was a train of six or seven small coaches standing in the station, with access from a stepped concrete platform. The coaches were all of steel, about ten feet long and with a bent-plate roof and open sides. Each car had four uphill-facing seats and we saw later that these would take three Japanese miners sitting abreast with ease under the low roof. However, there was much difficulty when we, mostly a foot taller than the Nips and new to the situation, tried to get in.

We were pushed in until all were aboard, with our heads between our knees and gasping for breath. We gathered that the contraption was called a *jin sha* (man carriage). When all the prisoners and their *buntai cho* were aboard and all projecting elbows, feet and knees had been pushed or kicked in, a loud bell sounded and a few seconds later we began our journey down the slope. I did not notice much on that first trip, except that we were following the strata of the rock.

It was not until later that I did some pulse counting and made estimates of speed, time and total depth. Almost exactly three minutes later, we reached the bottom of the run, having passed the ascending train at the halfway point, after which we had a walk of between four and five minutes along a horizontal tunnel, back to the top of a second *jin sha*. This was almost identical to the No. 1 and again took three minutes to descend.

After a short walk we came to our place of work, cutting a horizontal tunnel in carboniferous limestone and filling the spoil into very large steel trucks called *haku*. For some unexplained reason I have a very poor memory of the details of that work, my main recollections being of the hardness of it and the dust from the limestone.

We did not know the names of any of our *buntai cho* (section leaders) but very quickly the British and Australian prisoners gave them animal names as a means of identification. There was The Horse who had a long neck, The Bull who had a short one, The Fox, The Rat, and of course there was Four Eyes, a lugubrious character who wore big round glasses. My own lord and master, *nana buntai cho*, was dubbed The Pig because he had a pimple on the end of his nose which gave him a rather porcine look and, moreover, he grunted a lot. It was not until nearly a year later that he told me his name was Maeda. Actually, he said: Maeda-san, the equivalent of Mr. Maeda. Even in those days I knew that, as in the UK, it was not good form to add the word san but it was typical of The Pig. He made no attempt to bridge the language barrier and always appeared to be extremely impatient. He used only one near-English word: Speedo! and would shout it at frequent intervals. Even after only a few days down the mine I hated the work and most of all I hated that Speedo, speedo, *nana buntai cho*.

My 'diary', consisting of brief notes on assorted scraps of paper, shows that I worked two and a half ten day shifts at that face. The first was the Day Shift for which we left camp at 6 a.m. and returned at 4 p.m. The second was the Afternoon Shift, for which we left camp at 2 p.m. and returned at midnight. The third was the Night Shift for which we left at 10 p.m. and returned at 8 a.m. Half- way through that first spell on the Night Shift and working at the limestone face, I had a sudden attack of violent stomach pains and had to be helped out of the mine at the end of the shift. Arrived back in camp, someone took me to the sick room and soon I was being almost carried into the adjacent block where a kindly medical orderly, Corporal Williams, told me not to worry because I was now in hospital. The complaint was called pellagra diarrhoea, the result of vitamin deficiency, and for a week I had to crawl to a pot outside the room at least once every half-hour, day and night. The hospital block was nearly full of patients, mostly Dutchmen, and with the same complaint as me. Dr. Rappard did his best for all of us but, with next to no medicines, much of the cure came from his own persuasion and forceful but pleasant personality. Like some twenty or more men in the hospital at that time, I was so ill and nauseated that the mere thought of food, no matter how appetising, was completely revolting, and to eat any of the watery rice gruel being served to us was almost an impossibility. Thinking about it, I can still hear Dr. Rappard's voice saying to me: 'How many times, Rhodes?' to which I would reply; 'Don't know, Sir. About every half-hour, I suppose.' 'Are you eating anything?' and with a shudder I would shake my head. Then Dr. Rappard would kneel down on the mat, put his hands on my shoulders, stare straight at me with his piercing eyes and say: 'Rhodes, you must eat! Force yourself! No, better, persuade yourself. I know you can do it.'

Thus encouraged, as were many other men in similar straits, I did my best to eat and gradually, after some weeks, the violence of the diarrhoea subsided a little. Every day Dr. Rappard would make his rounds and ask each man the same question: 'Good morning, Rhodes. How many times?' 'Good morning, Sir. Twenty, I think.' 'Hmm,' and he would look at his notes. 'You were twenty-five yesterday. Are you feeling a little better?'

Some of the Dutchmen who had known him from earlier days called him 'The Bicycle Mender' but Dr. Rappard was really very popular and well respected by all. He stood up to the Japanese as well as he could, and even without medicines he must have saved the life of many a man, including me, simply by his force of character and his encouragement.

When one was so very ill, the only thing anyone wanted to do was to sleep, and even eating was a great effort. As to be expected, under those conditions all the men lost weight very rapidly. I had always been lightly built, had lost some weight in Changi, and should guess that I would have been about 8 stones, or 50kg, when I arrived in Japan. That would have been about average for the British party but some of the Australians might have been just a little heavier. I was put on the scales some three months after being taken ill and then recorded only 32.5 kg, or about 5 stones, 2lb.

Gradually, as the diarrhoea subsided, my appetite returned, even for plain boiled rice, and it was then that I began to notice that men who were not working down the mine received a reduced ration. However, the cooks were sometimes able to wangle a little more for those in hospital, and this would be delivered very quietly, usually in the late evening when there was least likelihood of Nip guards being around. About a month after I went into hospital some wheat flour was introduced into the rations, and then the miners had for one of their meals in camp a small loaf of bread which was about 8 inches long, about 3 inches wide, and 2 inches deep. I never knew its weight. I remember several occasions when, at about 11 p.m., there would be a quiet call of 'Psst!' outside the room. One of us would slide open the *shoji* (sliding screen) and one of the cooks, without a word, would throw four loaves into our room. Merely writing about it, even so many years later, reminds me vividly of the pleasure with which I tore off pieces of fresh bread and savoured every lovely mouthful. I also remember the feeling of continuing hunger and the sad resignation when the last morsel had gone.

Throughout the two and a half years of my stay in the mine camp we had an issue of toilet paper, three pieces each per person per day. This was immediately assessed as: one up, one down, and one polish, but in fact it was not quite like that because the paper was so flimsy as to be almost useless if used singly. Moreover, its wooden origins were all too obvious, although I never heard of anyone actually suffering from splinters. The ration was barely adequate for those who were not ill (I nearly wrote: those who were in good health), but clearly it was not so for those in the hospital block. So our captors generously gave us an increased ration of six sheets per day. Some men, particularly among the Dutch, used water from an old wine bottle, or from a small pot, but one Englishman in the next room to me found his own solution to the problem.

The hospital block was next to the high wooden fence on the western boundary of the camp, and separated from it by a cinder-covered pathway about 12'-wide. At some time before we arrived, someone had dug up a 2 feet wide strip along the fence and planted some castor oil bushes. As soon as our friend, a small Londoner with an ever present grin, was fit to walk a few yards, he would go quietly over to the fence and help himself to a couple of the big palmate leaves. For a period of about three months of that summer and autumn several of those castor oil plants looked distinctly bare.

As I became a little better I did not need to sleep all day, and time began to hang somewhat heavily. Conversation was the first need but that required that other men sharing the room were also feeling well enough to want to talk. All manner of subjects were discussed, one of the favourite subjects being our pre-war jobs. On many occasions when a man was describing some event or action from the past he would date it as 'last year', and then hastily correct himself, saying 'I mean in 1938'. We all tended to discount the time between call-up and the present, for most of us a period of about four years.

After the war I travelled a part of the way home with a man who boasted that he was almost unique in NOT having learned to play bridge while a POW. The fact is, of course, that he was far from unique, but yet many men did learn. A Dutchman in the same room with me and perhaps some twenty years older, Herman van Lennep, who had been a buyer for KPM, the Royal Dutch Passenger Fleet, taught me to play and also advocated the 'club convention'. He and I won many rubbers but there were never any stakes, simply because we had nothing with which to gamble. He had an Arts degree from Leiden and he was able to entertain us with his many reminiscences and philosophical theories.

A modest number of books had been brought into the camp and although reading was not to every one's taste they were a great deal read. I had had several books in Changi, mostly collected from the godowns in Singapore and 'paid for' by receiving the usual two clouts but I took only two to Japan. One was an American digest of classical essays and the other was '*Interior Decoration*' by Sherril Whyton. It too was American but was modelled almost exactly on the well-known '*History of Architecture*' by Bannister-Fletcher. It gave a very clear history of the development of interior decoration through the ages and also included separate chapters on such subjects as china, glassware, silverware, wallpapers, etc. From that description it does not sound like fascinating reading but yet I found it to be so, as did many other men when they got to hear about it. From the last months of 1943 until the end of the war in 1945, at frequent intervals different men, British, Dutch or Australian, would come to my room and ask, hopefully: 'Any chance of borrowing the book?' The reason for our derived enjoyment was simple. The book described in very readable prose, and with numerous illustrations, standards of living which were almost the antithesis of our present circumstances. If, on the radio programme: '*Desert Island Discs*' I were to be asked which book I should like to have with me, there could be no doubt about the answer, the choice coming from hard experience.

Once every ten-day shift we had a visit from the Japanese doctor from the mine hospital, an elderly man employed by the mining company. He would visit all the patients in what might have been called the 'surgical wards' but declined to go into the rooms where the sick were housed. However, every one who could walk a few yards had to line up on the cinder path in front of those castor oil plants and he would then inspect each of us. He was always accompanied by Dr. Rappard and by the Japanese medical orderly, a man whom I did not like and whose name, I later learned, was Yoshikawa.

If the mine doctor thought a man was really workable (not the same as fit to work), he would mutter the single word: *yama* (mine). Alternatively, if the man was not workable but still capable of going back to his billet and attending *tenko*, he would mutter two words: *renpei kyu* (parade class). Yoshikawa, however, with very little knowledge of English, had his own version of renpei kyu and put the man down as camp worker, which meant that one could still be worked very hard, so long as it was in the camp and not down the mine.

For the remainder, a collection of bedraggled wretches, the doctor would say nothing or would pause for a second look, then say: 'Ush. OK.' I had no inspection at all during the first month but then, over the next five months I survived about fifteen such parades. Being little more than skin and bone, I must have looked very feeble, and of course I did nothing to improve my appearance.

It was while I was in hospital that I began to lose my back teeth. They just crumbled and broke off, leaving the roots still there. The result was that I could not chew anything and had to do my best by eating like a rabbit with my front teeth. Fortunately, the rice and soup diet did not call for much chewing. Even more fortunately, I never had any pain from the remnant gums while I was a prisoner.

Autumn turned to winter and I was glad to be in the shelter of the hospital block, despite its limitations, but my luck ran out on 28th January 1944 when I was inspected and tagged as 'Camp worker'.

The latitude of Kitakyushu is about thirty-four degrees north, about that of Northern Morocco. When we arrived there in midsummer the weather was not quite tropical but still comfortably warm, and most of the ensuing winter was still quite mild. Sometimes, however, the wind blew from the north-west, bringing an uncomfortably cold blast straight out of north-east Asia.

Even in the billets we felt the cold because there was no heating and the windows, with their unputtied glazing, were of little protection against the strong north-westerly wind. It just whistled around the barrack blocks and found its way in anywhere it could. It was not until the second winter, at the end of 1944, that we were given some old newspapers and a small amount of rice flour paste and told to apply the paper where the putty should have been. We were not permitted to seal up the sliding panels in the upper rooms because the Nip guards wanted to be able to enter the rooms that way, from the first floor balcony. There was a hold-up in the next room to mine when it was discovered that one of the men had succumbed to hunger and eaten the paste!

The coal miners, dressed only in their skimpy work clothes, became surprisingly eager to get down the pit but we, the camp workers, had to spend the day trying to dodge that biting wind. We did not have to wear the work clothes but, having been prisoners in the tropics for a year, none of us had any really warm garments of any kind. One, a Dutch friend of mine, had brought an old British blanket with him. Having had some training as a tailor, he borrowed a pair of scissors and a needle, scrounged some thread and made himself a 'romper suit'. He must have been one of the warmest men in the camp.

On one occasion during that period as a camp worker there was a fall of snow. It is a comparative rarity in Kyushu and there was only about half an inch but its effect on the prisoners was interesting. Most of the British prisoners just cursed it. They were in no mood to make snowmen or to have snowball fights and it just meant that one had to put on boots to go to the mess room or to the latrines. Most of the prisoners had a pair of boots in addition to the split-toed ones issued by the mine company, and many also had a pair of wooden sandals, usually home made. These were of no protection against the snow and slush and one's feet soon became muddy and cold. But many of the Dutch contingent, having been born in Indonesia and never having left it, were most intrigued.

So was at least one well-spoken Englishman who, although he sometimes referred to 'back home', meaning England, apparently had never been far from Singapore. They were to be seen picking up the snow, looking closely at it and even licking it, However, next time it snowed they disliked it every bit as much as we did.

I suppose I was lucky to be put with a party of about twenty prisoners whose duty was to repair the rubberised boots worn by the miners. We sat on the matted floor around the walls of a large room next to where our belongings had been stored. The only equipment provided was some very large needles and some black thread, and there was only one pair of scissors between us. It was really a fruitless task because once the thin rubberised fabric had been punctured it tore very easily from that point. However, we felt that we had to do our best because the Nips had said that there were no more boots and we saw no reason to disbelieve them. The miners would just be left to get along with what they had. I was always reasonably adept with a needle, but it was clear that some of my companions were doing more harm than good.

The shoe mending party had been at work for some weeks before I joined them. A Dutch sergeant major, Kramer, welcomed me to the party and soon there was a lively chat going, with me, the only newcomer, as the centre of interest. This all helped to pass the time and enable us to forget the cold. It continued, with various subjects of conversation, for a few days until 'Stip' Kramer interrupted and spoke directly to me. Had I noticed, he asked, that we all were talking in English and yet I was the only Englishman present? He asked if I would mind if they reverted to speaking Dutch, on the understanding that they would help me along. I accepted the new challenge readily and we managed quite well but, for the record, I still cannot speak Dutch.

Two more medical inspections were passed satisfactorily with the repeat order of 'camp worker' but then, on 25th February 1944, I heard that dreaded word: *yama* (mine).

With considerable trepidation I got up next day, a Saturday, at 3 p.m. and dressed myself in the issued work clothes, filled my water bottle and went for breakfast with the afternoon shift. One small consolation was the well-filled bowl of rice and the amount that had been put in my *bento baku* (picnic lunch box). Although not by any means a good meal, it was nevertheless half as much more than I had been receiving as a camp worker.

I was once again under the command of The Pig, of Section 7, who clearly did not recognise me as having been with him some six months previously. He looked me up and down and it was plain that he did not at all like what he saw. He had a work schedule and wanted workers, not walking skeletons. Not that the other nine or ten men in the *buntai* were all that sturdy; one or two, including Fred Harrison who had been one of those who collapsed on the roadside and had been brought into camp the morning after we arrived, looked to me to be in very poor shape. However, to judge by The Pig's expression and his grunt of disgust, he thought I was the worst. He looked at the number on my little label and muttered: '*Hachi-ju genki nai!*' (Eighty not strong!).

We collected lamps, bowed to the kami on the hill, and entered the mine, but when we reached the bottom of the No. 2 *jin-sha*, I was surprised to find that we then had a long and rather twisting walk which lasted about twelve minutes. At the end we came to a third jin-sha. That one took all of ten minutes to descend and I later calculated that our depth below ground must be at least 5,000 feet. Once again we started to walk, but soon stopped at a small store where the Pig collected a large canvas bag of *maito* (dynamite), and the necessary detonators and firing mechanism. Meanwhile we picked up a metal bottle of oil for the jack-hammer, and a supply of *ebu* (baskets) and *kake-ita* (scrapers). At the bottom of the haulage run, up which trains of full coal trucks were taken, in a cavern-like enlargement of where the two tunnels met, were a number of empty trucks, called *haku*.

Those trucks, seen in the dim light from our cap lamps, looked huge and were indeed very heavy. They measured about 8 feet long, 4 feet wide and about two-and-a-half feet deep. Made of quite thick sheet steel, they were mounted on sturdy steel chassis projecting at each end as a snap coupler. There was also a chain link and hook. Their interior capacity would have been about 72 cubic feet and would have held about three and a half tons of small coal. The empty truck must have weighed at least half a ton.

The Pig set off to walk up the tunnel, carrying the explosives, while the prisoners collected empty trucks and, with two men to each, proceeded to push them up the track. We trudged with hands on the back of the truck, heads down so that our lamps lit up the rail and the ground, for what seemed like an eternity. In fact it was only about twenty minutes but my back and legs ached by the time we came to a halt. My fellow pusher, Joe Keen, warned me that we must keep going at a steady pace. If we went too slowly, our legs could be broken by the following truck, and if we went too quickly we could similarly hurt those in front. The tunnel was supported every metre by pieces of heavy railway line, spanning the tunnel between tree trunk posts at either side. Those 'arches' made very effective sound baffles so that one could not hear the rumble of the next truck, nor the voices of the pushers, even if they were only a few feet away

When I had a chance to glance around I saw that the tunnel appeared to be cut entirely within the depth of a thick coal seam. The seam dipped from left to right, presumably at the same angle and in the same direction as the *jin-sha* and haulage tunnels. The working tunnel had been cut more or less along the strike (contour) of the bed, but slightly to the left so as to climb slowly up hill. The effect of this was that while we had to push hard to get the empty trucks up to the face, when filled they could be expected to roll back down the gentle slope without effort. At least, that was the theory, but I soon discovered that, like a lot of things in Japan at that time, it did not always work.

Every day during that long push-up of the trucks the men would talk and the topic of conversation was always the same: food! Over all the years as a prisoner I tried to keep my mind concentrated on other things, and was grateful for the fact that I had never been a big eater, nor had any great love of food. But in those deprived conditions, food, and the memories of meals of previous days seemed to dominate my conscious thoughts. I hated the idea but talked just the same.

Someone banged on the truck and we stopped immediately, at our work place, the end of the tunnel. I looked up and saw that the large metal ventilation trunking, which had been slung above our heads, ended just in front of us. Walking forward past the three trucks in front of ours, I could see that the coal face at the end of the tunnel was covered to a depth of about five feet with a big pile of loose coal. The height of the tunnel was about seven feet and its width at the roof was about 8 feet, and 10 feet at the floor, and thus I guessed that the pile of coal must weigh about 20 tons.

Without delay the Pig had us at work. The jack-hammer and its long bit, and the pneumatic pick, were already at the face, left there by the preceding shift. I had not seen those men but on later days we usually passed them in the tunnel between the No. 1 and the No. 2 *jin-sha*. Two men were told to use the jack-hammer and the rest of us began to fill the trucks, beginning with the hindermost. Three of us scraped and filled the baskets while the rest formed a chain to pass the baskets back to the truck. When three of the big trucks had been filled, the Pig sent me and three others to take the first two filled trucks back down to the haulage run, and I was glad of the change of work. Having spent nearly three hours bent double and scraping away, my back was aching and so were the backs of my legs.

On that occasion, my first, the truck ran well for most of the way, requiring only a little pushing, and while it ran by itself we jumped on the rear end of the chassis. I quite enjoyed the ride although we had to keep a very attentive watch down the inky black tunnel to ensure that we did not run into the one ahead of us. Having left the full trucks at the siding whence we had collected them, the four of us walked back up to the face, but again we had to be alert in case the Pig had sent a third full truck down

When we returned to the face the Pig greeted us with a grunt and a bad-tempered: '*Jikan takusan*!' (A long time) and then shouted: '*Ush. Bento*!' (OK. Picnic lunch), whereupon he and some ten prisoners promptly sat down at the side of the tunnel to eat our rice. Our *bento* never varied but, as time passed, we could savour the rice and could tell if there had been a change of supply. Moreover, some boasted that they could tell which of the cooks had prepared it.

The Pig gobbled his rice very quickly, taking only a few minutes to empty his box but he allowed us to sit for about fifteen minutes before shouting: '*Ush. Shigoto!*' (Work!), when we perforce had to start work again. The two men with the jack-hammer had drilled the higher holes while able to stand on the heap, but now they had to drill the lower ones while we cleaned up the last of the loose coal. When the holes had been drilled and all the loose coal had been cleared away, the explosive charges were inserted and it was always the Pig who handled the *maito*.

Except for the group up near the roof, all the holes had two sticks of dynamite, but the central upper group had only the one. The detonators were pushed into the outer sticks, each complete with about one-and-a-half metres of trailing wire and then, with a long wooden rod, the maito was pushed to the full depth of the hole and followed by two or three little sausages of hand-rolled clay. That lot filled about half of the metre-long hole, the remainder being filled up with well-tamped damp sand. The Pig then wired them up in three groups, the first to be fired being three on the centre line near the floor. The second firing was of the two side groups, and the final one was the holes up near the roof.

During the firing we all retreated down the tunnel for a distance of about thirty feet. At first I thought that we were still too close, but then the bangs were much less than I expected, the sound being baffled by the arches. On only one later occasion did a single piece of coal land about a yard short of the nearest man.

The last job of the shift was to erect the next arch. The two side posts, called *waku ashi*, were about ten inches in diameter, the left hand side one being about seven feet long while the other was about two feet longer. The aim was to have both posts founded on the shale rock underlying the coal, while having the tops level, and to achieve this we had to dig a hole in the floor for the right hand one. The top of each post was notched to take the end of the railway line, this rather expert work with an axe always being done by the Pig.

Erection of the arch was always hard work, simply because of the weight of the steel bar and of the tree trunks at each side. To get the bar into position and tight against the roof entailed lifting and holding it above our heads. Its weight would have been about 260 lb (118 kg) and we were lucky if we could have four men to do the lifting. Usually, the Pig would allow only three men to do the lifting, the rest being needed to hold the heavy side posts. There never was an accident in *nana buntai*, at least not while I was there, but we heard of other groups who did drop the bar, causing broken legs and crushed feet. It is now amusing, in a wry way, to think that the total weight of the three men doing the lifting was probably less than the weight of that piece of old railway line!

I worked at that face for nearly a month, first on the afternoon shift for nine days, then, after a rest day, another nine days on nights. It was three days into the day shift on the 20th March and near finishing time when I had a sudden terrible pain in the sole of my left foot. A piece of sharp coal had entered my foot via a hole in my boot and an abscess had developed very quickly. In our extremely debilitated state that was what usually happened. A scratch in the morning was septic, red and swollen by evening.

My foot swelled as I watched it and at going home time I was limping so badly that I only just caught the last of three trains on the lowest or No. 3 *jin-sha*. Then there was the long walk around to No. 2 and again I only just caught the last run. By the time I had hobbled round to the No. 1 *jin sha* the last train had gone, the 'station' lights (all two of them) were out and I perforce had to walk up. Now that would have been quite a task for a fit man because the slope was more than one in two and the floor was strewn with slippery slabs of shale, but for an underfed five-and-a-half stone weakling with an abscess on one foot, it was an horrendous experience. When eventually I emerged from the *jin-sha* house, more than two hours late, the Pig was there alone and waiting for me. He grabbed me by the ear, muttering all the time: '*Hachi-ju joto nai!*' (Eighty no good!) and dragged me, still by the ear, all the way back to the camp, where he kicked impatiently at the gate. When it was opened by a soldier, the Pig stuffed me through without a word, turned on his heel and went home, presumably to a cold bath and a cold supper.

The soldier ordered me to attention then gave me a couple of hard clouts to the head, after which he ordered me to the *o-furo* (bath house). I explained as well as I could that first I needed to collect a change of clothes and then, after washing, I urgently needed to go to the sick room. Rather grudgingly, the soldier assented, waited while I washed and then took me to the sick room. I had hoped to find Dr. Rappard but he was away, probably in the mess room, and the only persons in attendance were Suidema, an Indonesian Dutch medical orderly, and Yoshikawa, the Nip medical orderly. The Nip signed that I should sit on a high couch and he then examined my left foot, which by that time was very swollen. I tried to explain that the cause of the trouble was in the sole but he ignored me, took an unsterilised scalpel and slashed across the top of my foot, looking quite disappointed when all that appeared was a lot of blood. Suidema bandaged it up and then gave me a drink of a teaspoonful of industrial alcohol in about five of water and asked the Nip where I should go. I was more than relieved when he replied: '*Ush! Byoin!*' (OK, Hospital!).

I was in the hospital block for two weeks, the first few days with a roaring temperature to go with the sore foot, by that time hurting on top as well as in the sole. Dr. Rappard saw it the next day, shrugged his shoulders as we exchanged a meaningful glance and a nod in the direction of the Nip, and gave me a few grammes of sulphonylamide, not on the wound but to take internally. The crystals came from an American field dressing.

I did another two weeks as camp worker and on two or three occasions went outside with a small party looking for dandelions for the Camp Commandant's rabbits. I enjoyed the sorties although they were not a good idea while my foot was not completely healed.

Down the pit again on the 19th April 1944, I was once again on the day shift but no longer working on the old tunnel. Instead, my section was working in a *nobori*, (from the Japanese verb *noboru*, to climb or ascend). It was a link tunnel driven up the slope of the stratum to join our original tunnel to another one running parallel to it but some hundred or so feet up the slope. Needless to say, those sloping tunnels were known to the POWs as 'Nobodies'. The work was both hard and dangerous. The drilling had to be done with all the holes angled upwards at about thirty degrees and with the heavy jack-hammer often held high above our heads. I spent several days on the drill and it was hell. Because of the sloping and slippery base, the heap of coal blown down did not stay in place to provide support for the drillers' feet and we found it exceedingly difficult to stay near the drill, let alone to press hard upon it. The pressing was essential, not only to drive the bit forward but also to minimise the violent recoil from the hammer.

If the team was drilling away quite satisfactorily and then, suddenly, one of the two drillers were to slip and to relax his pressure, the other man could suffer quite severe bruising, depending upon which part of one's anatomy was pressing on the back of the hammer. A cushion of flesh was needed but we, being so scraggy, could find very few places where the bones were not uncomfortably near the surface. I hated that bloody drill!

The empty trucks were lined up in the lower tunnel and the loose coal at the face was first scraped into baskets and then thrown into a V-shaped sheet steel trough down the centre line of the sloping shaft. In the trough it was then pushed down to the bottom by men using long poles. Finally, at the bottom of the chute it was again basketed and thrown into the truck. The danger arose because it was almost impossible to see properly when throwing the coal into the chute, and all too often big pieces missed their target and came bouncing down the slope, invisible in the darkness. Moreover, if the jack-hammer was in use, the clattering noise completely swamped any sound from the bouncing coal. With no muffling at all and with its exhaust only inches from one's face, I was quite deaf for a few days after first using it, but eventually became accustomed to it so that some sort of conversation with one's fellow driller was even possible. However, since then I have had tinnitus, an everlasting singing in the ears.

The erection of an arch was even more difficult in the nobori where, because of the slope, the heavy metal bar had to be lifted so that its bottom was more than seven feet above the ground, and just about the limit for a tall man standing on tiptoe.

On the last day of May and four days into the afternoon shift, when I was using a long pole on the coal in the trough, a big piece came flying down and hit my right shin. The thin puttees were no protection and my flesh was burst open at the shin bone. The next day I was again in hospital and spent eleven days there

Back down the mine on the 12th June and on night shift, I found to my great relief that the *nobori* had been completed up to the next level, and *nana buntai* was back working in the original tunnel. By that time our numbers were down to about eight and as I was one of the tallest I was all too often detailed to work the jack-hammer, but with different partners. There were at least two men with whom I preferred not to work because they cheated in that they would pretend to push but then did not take their proper share.

One of them even stole my picnic lunch, and presumably ate it in one of the nobori because that is where the empty box was found. Actually, the *nobori* were not very pleasant places. There were air locks at each end, from the main tunnels they joined, the reason being that otherwise they would interfere with the ventilation. The air in them was always stale and usually distinctly tainted, the reason being that they were often used as toilets.

Some members of my section were not only physically sick and generally debilitated, but also were not very bright mentally. One day the Pig remarked to me on the fact, saying (or signing) that he could only rely on three men: 421 (Cpl. Frank Jones), 480 (PSR), and 481 (Joe Keen). To that list I would have added the name of Jack Kant, whose number I forget, but I had to agree about the present unreliability of the other four or five. I think that the Pig knew that this was the result of their privations and certainly not wilful stupidity, but he was expected by his bosses, the mine managers, to produce coal commensurate with the number of men in his care. Even at that time, deep in the pit and loathing the work, I recognised that there was really no personal animosity from the Pig, and on more than one occasion I heard a fellow prisoner sum him up as: 'Oh, the Pig's all right!' All the same, I hated him.

Joe Keen was about two years older than me and had been a civil servant in the motor transport department of Johore State. He returned to England after the war, but died some time later of cancer of the bowel. He and I worked well together on the jack-hammer.

Frank Jones was about the same age as me and had been a copy typist for a Fleet Street news agency. He was nominated as the leader of our *buntai* and the Pig would summon him if he needed men to do a particular task, but it was Frank who might receive the first clout if the Pig was not satisfied with the result. I liked Frank Jones.

One day when most of the heap had been scraped up it was seen that a small block of coal at the lower left hand had not been displaced by the dynamite and so the Pig told me to take the pneumatic pick and to remove it. I was doing this very carefully when a large sheet of coal about six inches thick peeled away from the left wall and fell on me. The Pig saw the fall, with me under it, and as I scrambled out and to my feet he shouted: '*Baka, omae wa, hachi-ju!*' (Fool, thou. Eighty!) He took a swipe at me with the basket he just happened to be holding. I dodged back but the basket caught and cut my right ear, and also knocked my already battered spectacles off into the darkness. As soon as the Pig realised that my spectacles had gone he was down on his hands and knees, looking for them. He found them quite easily and, equally fortunately, they were unbroken. He then fussed about seeing them safely back on my nose, but was not at all interested in the blood which was streaming from my right ear, and also from my left hand and shoulder, the result of the fall. I still have traces of the blue marks left behind where the coal dust got into the cuts, and even now my right ear tends to bleed, particularly in winter.

On another occasion during that period I was busy inserting and wedging short pieces of small poles behind the big side-posts to hold up the coal at the side of the tunnel. My thoughts were far away when suddenly the Pig came up behind me and hit me several times around the head. He grabbed me by the shoulder and spun me round to face him, then put his dirty hand over my mouth and shouted: '*Kichibue ga kinjiru desu!*' For a moment I had no idea what was wrong. Something was *kinjiru* (forbidden), but what? Then the Pig took his hand from my mouth, puckered up his own lips and said: '*Kichibue! Kichibue wo fuku!*' The penny dropped. I had been whistling under my breath. The Pig went on to explain, using signs and grunts and a lot of Japanese which I didn't understand. If anyone whistled down the mine, the *kami sama* (guardian spirit) up in the mountain would *okotte iru*, (be angry) and, far more to the point, the roof might come in. I nodded quickly, saying '*Hai. Wakarimasu*' (Yes. I understand).

I should have liked to be able to tell him that I always wanted to whistle, albeit under my breath. It had been a lifelong habit and I had often got into trouble at school for whistling in class. I should have liked to be able to explain many other things as well, but how could one? As discovered in Singapore, language is one of the greatest barriers to friendship and the cause of a large portion of the world's strife. Also, as I was to discover later, it can be a real key to the magic world of discovery, friendship and adventure.

I swear I had not been whistling, or at least I don't think I had, when a few days later the roof of the tunnel did fall in. It was about a hundred yards back from the face and we only discovered it when we walked back, pushing our full trucks at the end of the shift. We had had a warning about half an hour previously, when the air supply stopped; although that had happened on a previous occasion as the result of trouble with the pumps.

Over a length of three arches, a distance of about ten feet, a four foot thickness of roof had come down and filled the tunnel with huge slabs of flaky shale. At first sight there was no way through but more careful peering upwards indicated that probably there was room to crawl over the top of the heap. However, when this was suggested to the Pig he would not hear of the idea. Instead, he made us sit down at the side of the tunnel and facing away from the fall, and then told us to keep absolutely quiet.

The Pig turned his cap around so that its beam, unlike ours which gave a general spread of light, was directed back and away from the fall while he kept a careful watch for any flash of an approaching light. We, facing away from the fall, strained to catch any sound of approaching conversation. It was some twenty minutes later that we heard the sound of voices, then silence, followed by a rather faint Japanese voice calling: '*Aw! Iru-ka?*' (Hi! Are you there?) The Pig called back and they exchanged comments, after which he said we must sit down and wait quietly until more help arrived. It seemed like ages but was probably about three-quarters of an hour before another call came.

There was no serious shortage of oxygen but without the *fu kan* (wind box or trunking) to bring us cool air the temperature had risen rapidly and we were all sweating very freely, although, so far as I could see, everyone was completely calm.

Eventually the Pig told us to climb up and over, one by one, and warned us to move as slowly and silently as possible. I was fifth or sixth to go, putting my feet exactly where Tthe Pig indicated as I clambered to the top of the heap. Pausing for just a second or two on the top, I could see that where I was sitting was about a foot higher than the normal roof level. The fall had left a roughly conical hole with its apex about four feet above my head, that is to say about seven feet above the ordinary roof level. All looked safe except for one very big slab of shale about a foot thick which was wedged at a very uncertain angle and close to my left ear. I slid down the slabs on the far side, helped by the hands of the Jap section leader who was squatting on the slope, and then was helped by the Dutchmen of the next shift. The Pig was the last to come over, and we watched as he and the other buntai cho bowed formally to each other. Feeling the urge to say something, I hung back and shook the hand of the other Nip, saying: '*Arigato*' (Thanks). He seemed quite surprised but then grinned broadly and said something which I didn't understand. With later knowledge it probably was: '*Do itashimashite*' (Not at all)

It was then that I noticed more bright lights shining on us and I saw several other Nips, the extra help who, presumably, had dragged down some of the larger slabs that had been on top of the pile. A dangerous job, I thought. I don't know who cleared the fallen rock away. I suppose that both the other shifts had worked hard at it, and repair gangs must have been in as well. When our next shift came around, only hours later, the tunnel was quite clear, the air trunking had been repaired and the roof where the fall had occurred was timbered.

My 25th birthday arrived on the 8th July 1944 but the only celebration was that I went on sick parade to complain about the reappearance of ulcers on my legs. Dr. Rappard said he could do little for me and as my temperature was normal Yoshikawa insisted that I should continue down the mine. I worked for another nine days but by that time the ulcers were much worse and I felt dizzy and generally ill. The feeling of pressure behind my ears led me to suppose that my temperature was up and, when I reported to the sick room, that proved to be so. Dr. Rappard appealed to Yoshikawa and, much to my relief, he agreed: '*OK, Byoin*' (OK, Hospital). That was on the 17th July and I was nominally in hospital but by that time so many men were ill that my 'bed' was a bare trestle table in a concrete floored storeroom. It was exceedingly uncomfortable, particularly as there was almost no flesh on my bones, but yet it was better than being down the pit.

I began to worry when, about five days later, I was sure that my temperature was back to normal. I did not have access to a thermometer but knew that the dizziness and the sense of pressure behind the ears had gone, yet the ulcers were still open and suppurating. With the next visit from the mine doctor drawing near, something had to be done. Then I came up with an idea and, three days later, it worked. The Nip doctor was able to take from me a thermometer which showed about 38 degrees Celcius or just over 100 degrees Fahrenheit. I used the same trick twice but then, with healed ulcers, was sent back to the mine and to the day shift on the 22nd August.

What I had done was to ask a friend to bring from my kit a Changi-made pipe which was then filled with tobacco from two cigarettes. I waited until the doctor was in the offing before lighting it, then when Suidema, the Dutch medical orderly, handed me a thermometer, I warmed up my finger and thumb on the pipe and gently massaged the thermometer until it read the desired 38 degrees.

The Pig welcomed me back to the buntai with a nod and a grunt and I struggled through two days of day shift, very glad that the third one was a rest day. The struggling was because although I felt reasonably well and fit (comparatively speaking), my legs and particularly my knees and ankles were hopelessly weak. Even the shared pushing up to the face of the empty truck was a great effort and I recall apologising to Jack Kant, my partner on the second day. After the rest day we changed to the afternoon shift and I got a full truck stuck in a dip in the track and had to trudge back to the face to ask for help. The Pig sent another man with me but not before giving me a good wallop and shouting the now all too frequently heard complaint: '*Hachi-ju joto nai!*' (Eighty no good!). The same thing happened on the next day when two of us were sent. We struggled for some time but could not push it out of the dip and The Pig was absolutely furious when, some time later, he came to look for us and, more importantly from his viewpoint, to look for the empty truck we were supposed to bring back.

When, at midnight, we returned to camp, the Pig reported to the guardroom and then came back to escort me, with a firm grip on my arm, to the sick room. I expected the place to be deserted but to my surprise Yoshikawa was there. The Pig told him a long tale, of which I understood only a word or two, and then Yoshikawa turned to me and, shouting in his very limited English, accused me of sabotage, repeating the word several times. I tried to deny the charge and explain that my legs were weak, but the Nip would hear none of it and was just about to administer the usual full-swing clout to the head when, to my surprise, the Pig interceded. So far as I could gather he said that I had been a good worker but now was too weak to do the work and if he was to produce his quota of coal he could not do it with sick men. Yoshikawa's arm stopped in mid-swing and he turned away abruptly, muttering: 'OK Camp Worker.' I breathed a sigh of relief and with a muttered 'Thank you' to Yoshikawa's back, I bowed politely to the Pig before limping back to my billet. I had finished with the Pig and with that ghastly mine.

I spent more than six months, from 26th August 1944 to 7th March 1945, as a camp worker, and while that meant being on only two thirds of the normal rations, for me it was much better than being down the mine. My first job was with the boot menders but that only lasted a couple of weeks, after which I was on general fatigues around the camp. The work itself was never a great problem but one met far too many young Nip guards, each of whom wanted to show his superiority by picking on any stray and single prisoner who happened to be around the camp. It was very difficult to avoid at least one good beating up each day.

Then, about the middle of October 1944, I was ordered to report to the guardroom. I expected trouble but when I arrived I was handed a brush and told to sweep. Thereafter, and for the next four months or so I reported every morning to the guardroom. One fellow prisoner, a middle-aged Australian named Jim Hope, erstwhile planter in Malaya, was already there as a clerk. He had been wounded and had difficulty in walking. Another prisoner, Jim Warner, had also been wounded and he was there as a general help. I became the 'dogsbody'. The Nip soldiers, under the command of a *gunso* called Takahashi, would tease me and I found that the best defence was to pretend to be simple. That earned me a lot of ridicule but no beatings, and sometimes I was given food and the occasional cigarette. I soon became known to all the Nips in the guardroom, including Lt. Suematsu, the Camp Commandant, as '*Megane baka*' (Bespectacled fool). I tried to listen to all conversations and although understanding only a little, nevertheless I was able to pick up the occasional bit of news, although it was clear that the Nips were poorly informed about the progress of the war. There was always the feeling that one was fooling around with one's head in the lion's mouth, but it passed the time, I was not getting the daily bashing, and I learned a little more of the language.

From time to time I was told to join the party going out to forage for rabbit food, but on a few occasions Takahashi, the Guard sergeant, led his own party. He always picked the biggest and strongest men available (what a false impression that statement creates!), and we were given two large coils of old but strong rope. Takahashi's aim, which he achieved only after several sorties, was to find and to drag into camp several large and weathered boulders, of which at least two must have weighed between one and a half and two tons. When the required number had been dragged in and left at the side of the parade ground, more or less opposite to the guard room, Takahashi again summoned a gang of camp workers. Then, with wooden poles and the ropes, we had to lift, arrange and set all those stones within a circle of some ten feet in diameter. As each stone was set, accompanied by much grunting and groaning from the prisoners, more or less in the positions he had indicated, with some on end and others lying flat, the sergeant walked round the circle, viewing the arrangement from every angle. Then, with his own grunts and gestures, he would have us move a stone just a little distance this way or that until he was quite satisfied. Finally, the cinder gravel round the stones was raked and encircled with a ring of stones, each about as big as a football. After one or two minor adjustments, Takahashi looked at his 'stone garden' and with great satisfaction in his voice, said: '*Ush. OK!*' He then turned on his heel and walked back to the guard room. At that time I had never heard of ikebana (flower arrangement) or its derivatives, nor had I heard of the stone gardens such as at Ryoanji in Kyoto, but I had to admit that Takahashi's stone garden was a near perfect work of art, showing harmony and balance when viewed from any angle.

About the end of February 1945 rumours went round the camp to the effect that a new *buntai* was to be formed from the camp workers. Further rumours said that those chosen would receive three quarter rations instead of the present two thirds. In fact the new section, called *gara buntai* although we never knew the meaning of the word *gara*, was formed on the 8th March 1945, with about twenty-five walking-sick prisoners. I cannot remember the exact personnel but there would have been some sixteen or seventeen Dutch and eight or nine British, myself included. When the day shift had gone to the mine we, a very ragged company of misfits, marched, or rather shambled, out of the gate and down the road towards the mine, but soon turned off to the left and onto a large area of coal washings just outside the camp. Our work was to make *mame tan* (bean coal), known in the UK as 'ovoids'; but just putting the coal dust through the machine which compressed and shaped the ovoids was not sufficient. The reason was that domestic fireplaces, complete with flue and chimney, were quite unknown in Japan and consequently the only fuel which could be burned in the little braziers, called hibachi, was either coke or charcoal. Therefore the ovoids had to be converted to coke. The coal mud was dug out of the big tip, using western-style spades, and was taken, in small tipper trucks on easily moveable light track, to the ball-making machine. From there the pressed ovoids were taken, by the same method, to some hard, flat ground on the mine side of the mud and near to the road, where they were tipped out. However, before the tipping, about one truckload was ignited in a big oil drum and, when well alight, the burning ovoids were carried by the shovel-full and laid on the ground in a long line of fire. Then the wagons of ovoids were tipped over the burning ones to form heaps of thirty or forty feet long, of triangular cross section, about four feet wide at the base and about two feet tall.

The heap was allowed to burn through for a time varying from half an hour to a full hour, depending on the force of the wind, and was then covered completely with three or four inches of damp coal mud, also brought up in the little trucks. That, the most important part of the operation, cut off the supply of air so that the heap slowly cooked itself into coke. On the next day but one, when the heap was cool, the local housewives came with buckets and bought the finished product. I have no idea of the actual costs but it seemed to be a simple and reasonably economic exercise.

Although the work was still moderately heavy, the pressure on us was much less than in the mine and we were allowed a rest in the middle of the morning and afternoon, as well as for *bento* (picnic lunch) at around midday. When we first began that work the only shelter was a small corrugated iron hut, close to the burning area, which contained the big oil drum. The weather could still be cold in March and so at break times all of us, and the three Nips, would crowd into the hut. The Nip who appeared to be both the brains and the boss was a studious looking fellow of about fifty. He had all the mannerisms of a civilian except for his walk, which was the stomping gait so characteristic of the ex-soldier. His deputy was a man of even greater years but obviously of less authority, and he too walked with a stomp. The third Nip was a young lad of about seventeen who, never having been a soldier, walked normally.

At rest times the prisoners would tend to gather in small groups but, as usual, I always wanted to try to talk with the Japanese and I found the young lad to be the most willing. At first when I approached him he cast a doubtful and questioning look at his seniors, deep in conversation, but the boss, whom we had soon dubbed: 'Four Eyes', just nodded and went on chatting. After that, conversation was possible on many days until the lad left us, and by that means I was able to enlarge my vocabulary, though not my understanding of the Japanese grammar.

One day away back in April or May of 1944, when *nana buntai* had been working on the *nobori*, we were marching from camp to mine in the early morning when someone remarked about the lush spring growth of the wild plants beside the road. We all glanced casually at it, but Harry Arnold, erstwhile agricultural worker from Dedham, remarked without any emphasis other than that of his local accent: 'That's Fat Hen. You can eat it.' At once at least a dozen voices demanded urgently: 'EAT WHAT?' Of course we could do nothing about it then because we were always under close escort when passing that spot, and soon the incident was forgotten. However, a year later, in the spring of 1945, the Fat Hen had grown up again and as it was only yards from our burning ground I and several other prisoners found opportunities to pick the leaves. I found an old tin can and, with a little water from my bottle, the Fat Hen was cooked over the remnant fire in the hut. I found to my delight that the resulting dark green vegetable was very palatable, being rather like spinach but better because it did not have the characteristic earthy taste. Not everyone liked the Fat Hen but I am sure that those of us who did eat it benefited from that wild spinach.

Incidentally, I saw civilian Nips, working on various surface jobs, collect fat caterpillars and roast them over their fires. It was intriguing to watch the use of *hashi* (chopsticks) at least three feet long and made from twigs cut from bushes nearby. I tried the caterpillars on one or two occasions when they were proffered by the Nips, and they were not at all bad although one could easily be revolted if one thought too much about it. I also tried snake once and found it to be quite tasty but glutinous and chewy. I was surprised to see the snake caught and eaten because, from experience in Singapore, I had thought that the Japanese were rather scared of them. In fact, in the days when I was in The Great World, if ever we were working at inland godowns and there was any long grass or bushes around, we had only to slash at the vegetation and all the Nips in the vicinity, at the shout of *hebi* (snake), would stop and join in the slashing. We gained many a rest by that ruse, but I never saw it used in Japan.

About a month after starting work in gara buntai, on a date later identified as the 13th April 1945, as we shambled back to camp we were met by children who danced alongside us, gleefully shouting: '*Ruzuberuto shinda! Ruzuberuto shinda!*' At first I did not understand but then the penny dropped. We were being told that Roosevelt was dead. The children and a few adults in the vicinity seemed to expect us to burst into tears and were quite disappointed when we just grinned. Nobody thought to tell us the news which later filtered through via the guardroom. The war in Europe was over and Hitler too was *shinda*.

One rest day at the end of July 1945, all the prisoners including the sick were taken across the front of the coal washings and then up the hill to behind the mine hospital building which was on higher ground between the coal washings and the mine head. There we found the entrance to a tunnel cut into the sandy rock of the line of hills to the north of the camp. The column of nearly a thousand prisoners was halted on the hillside and the Camp Commandant then explained that, as we might have American air raids, this was a shelter specially prepared for us. (True, we had seen the occasional plane flying over at great height.) The head of the column was then ordered to march in until the leaders emerged at the far end of what was obviously a U-shaped tunnel, when they were told to back up a little, by which time I was still waiting to go in.

The soldiers then began to shout and push until all of us were within the tunnel, and by that time we were squashed together and standing chest to back. As it happened, I was one of the last to go in and therefore was close to the entrance when I heard the Camp Commandant ask the Mine Manager how the entrance would be closed. He was shown, and I saw, the shot holes already drilled for the charges that would be used to blow up the openings. Then I understood! If an invasion, not an air raid, were to come, we all should be marched and crammed into that tunnel - and that would be end of us! 'Oh, no, Mr. American; no prisoners here!' I'm very glad there was not an invasion!

On that same rest day and after we all had returned to camp, I went to the camp barber for a shave and a hair cut. There had been rumours and speculation that Japan, by then the sole survivor of the Axis Powers, was losing battles in the Pacific. The information, such as it was, came from the guardroom via Jim Hope or Jim Warner, or from remarks made by the Commandant to Lt. Slieuw, and there were other small signs. Sergeant Takahashi, once feared for his irascibility, had suddenly become quite polite and had suggested a few changes to improve our well-being. Of course he could not increase the food rations but his efforts were welcomed. However, Lt. Sliew did comment to me that he thought Takahashi was 'buying himself an insurance policy'.

Although without real foundation, there was a growing feeling that, as Dr. Nairnsey, the South African, said: 'We're going home soon!' Having asked for a hair cut, I remarked rather casually to the Dutch barber: 'Please forget the top. Just trim the back and sides.' 'Ja?' asked the barber, but he said no more and did as requested.

There was nothing at all unusual about Wednesday, the 15th August 1945 when the day started. In fact it is doubtful if anyone in our camp could have told the date at the time. I ate the usual inadequate breakfast of a three-quarter full bowl of rice and a bowl of watery vegetable soup and had the same quantity of rice put into my lunch box. Then I fell in for roll call on the parade ground and watched most of the British and Australian party march out for the day shift down the mine. Then, with the other twenty-five or so walking sick, I was marched out and round to the coal ball plant.

It was a hot day and the morning dragged on in its usual weary way and then we all went into the hut to eat our picnic lunch. The hut had been erected a few months previously on the north side of the washings and quite close to the north- east corner of the camp, inside which was the cookhouse. The hut had only two windows, both of which were unglazed and at the back. We prisoners sat on seats around the walls of the larger, left-hand room, while the three Nips had a seat in the smaller, right hand room and facing their window. Judging by the position of the shadow of the corner of the hut in relation to several stones which we had 'accidentally' left lying around, the time was about 2 p.m. We had eaten our lunch and all, including the Nips, were snoozing when I heard an American voice calling from the direction of the cookhouse: 'Say! Is anyone there?' No one else appeared to be awake so I got up and walked across to look out of our window. One of the cooks had his head stuck out between the boards at the corner of the fence, and he waved to me. 'I don't know how true it is,' he said, 'but we've just heard that the war ended at noon today.' 'Oh, thanks!' I replied. I waved and sat down again. We had heard that story before and there seemed to be no reason to lose good snoozing time just for another rumour. However, one of the Dutchmen, a half-caste Indonesian, who was only about 'ninepence in the shilling', had also heard the American and he began to shout somewhat hysterically: 'What's that? What's that? War ended?...' I told him to shut up but his voice had woken the others and so we had a quick conference in muted voices.

The most senior rank present was Sergeant Major 'Stip' Kramer and he gave good counsel. 'It may be true but we do not know. We have heard this before. If it is true we shall know soon enough. I think we should look after the present, so let us keep quiet and not waken the Japs.' This advice was readily accepted and we all dozed on until about a quarter of an hour later when I heard footsteps round the back of the hut, and the head of a Nip I did not know appeared above our window sill.

Seeing only prisoners, he walked on and looked into the Nips' room. From where I was sitting I could see almost all of the window through the connecting doorway. The newcomer called to his friends: 'Are you there?' 'Yes. What is it?' came the sleepy reply. 'Have you heard?' 'No. Heard what?' 'The war's over'.

Immediately there was a scramble as all three rushed to the window. 'Who's won?' I could see a three-quarter view of their eager faces. 'America', came the reply. 'Saa...', and I could see the faces drop. There was silence for quite a while, except for some heavy sighs, then: 'Are you sure?' 'Yes, it's true. I heard it just now on a radio at the mine.' I was fascinated to see the way in which our three Nips visibly wilted. All four stood without saying anything more for some time, and then the visitor said he must go, and our three went back to their bench.

I had been so absorbed with listening to the Japanese conversation that it was only when the little scene had ended that the truth dawned upon me. The war really was over and the arrogant Nips had been beaten. I sat for a while to adjust my thoughts, then I walked over to wake Stip and to tell him the good news, and soon we all knew. Surprisingly, there was a great calm and even our excitable friend was quiet. After a while Stip spoke in a very soft voice. The war really was over, he said, and the Japs had been beaten, but we should now be very very careful. They could turn nasty without warning and we had no defence at all. We were all sick men and so perhaps we should just sit quietly and pretend that we knew nothing. Stip's advice was again accepted but there was a buzz of conversation as each of us developed his thoughts, arising out of the sudden realisation that there might be a future for us after all.

At least another half-hour passed and then, at about three o'clock, our three came stomping out of their room, shouting: '*Ush. Shigoto! Shigoto!*' That was the last thing they should have said to us. We were in no mood to 'Work! Work!' any more, and someone shouted back: '*Shigoto Nai. Senso wa owari.*' (No work. War finished'). All three began to shout: '*Owari nai!*' and they began to hit us with their sticks. I could see that all three had been weeping and that they were now putting on a show. We outnumbered them but the hut was rather small, and there could have been great danger if we had put up a fight. At a word from Stip we moved out onto the coal mud and scattered as widely as possible so that the Nips could not control us all at once. One of the Nips was more aggressive than the others and there was very nearly a fist-fight but some of us moved quickly to intercept our English colleague and it came to nothing. Then Four Eyes led a small group of us to a flat area of mud near the road, took a spade from someone and dug a clod of the black mud which he then threw as far away as he could manage, challenging us to beat his throw. That eased the tension and soon we were all playing the game, carefully allowing the Nips to do better than us. That went on for another half-hour until one of the guards from the camp came round to us. Apparently he brought official orders and soon we were being marched back to camp.

Our little party, all classed as sick or disabled in some way, were not good at marching, but as a matter of pride we did our best. When we were in the camp, instead of the Nip escort giving the order to halt and to salute the guardroom, it was Stip who called in English: 'Halt,' and then instead of the usual Japanese order of 'Left Turn. Salute' he just said in a loud clear voice: 'Dis-miss!'

There was a cheer and our little party ran or hobbled away to our various billets, without so much as a glance at the guardroom. So ended my working days in Japan.

CHAPTER EIGHT

A MONTH OF FREEDOM IN JAPAN

After a visit to the bath house, we spent the next two hours or so sitting in our various rooms, just talking about what we hoped to do when we got back home. Suddenly someone realised that the day shift would soon be returning and that, in all probability, they would not have heard the good news. About eight of us, mostly British, gathered at the side of the parade ground and just out of sight of the guard room.

Sure enough, a few minutes later the gates were opened by one of the guards and in marched the day shift, mostly British and Australian, under the escort of their various buntai cho, and they were halted in front of the guardroom. That was our cue and before the next order could be given we were dancing amongst them, shaking hands and shouting the news. 'The war's over! The war's over!' There was no angry shout of '*Kura!*' from the guard room. In fact there was not a Nip soldier in sight. About a hundred and fifty men just stood around in little groups, talking excitedly for what seemed ages until some of the miners realised that they were very tired, very dirty, and very hungry. The evening meal was still the same as usual except that all the bowls were filled to the top with rice, that being the best the cooks could do at the time.

I didn't sleep at all that night as the six men in our upstairs room talked until dawn. Next day, the 16th August, we stayed in camp and changed barrack blocks so as to regroup ourselves into national units instead of the working party groups as ordained by the Nips. Unfortunately, the block I had left was reasonably clean, whereas the one in which I then found myself was not. As soon as the night came, so did the bed bugs. That block was alive with the smelly little beasts and so for the second night I got no sleep On the 17th a big American bomber flew high above us and dropped a single parachute which landed just outside our camp. I have no idea what, if anything, had been attached to the 'chute but I joined a scrimmage for bits of it as souvenirs, coming out bruised but triumphant with some nylon webbing which, several years later, my wife wore as a belt.

The 18th was again spent in camp, amid great uncertainty. No one knew what was happening, not even the Japanese soldiers still living in the guardroom. The Commandant had gone to his home on the other side of the village, leaving Sergeant Takahashi in charge. As I walked past the guardroom one of the guards, recognising me as *Megane Baka*, (the bespectacled fool) who once had swept out their rooms, half smiled at me and so I walked up the steps to him, trying to look as if I owned the place. He smiled again, and offered me a cigarette which I accepted with thanks, and I then went on to comment on the weather, all in Japanese. Two more of the guards joined us and I made more remarks about the general situation. Wouldn't they like us, hope to go home soon?

There was no answer from any of them, not because they didn't understand but because their mouths were hanging open! I must admit to deriving great satisfaction from that moment as the truth about their *Megane Baka* dawned upon them. However, as my ability to understand quickly spoken vernacular Japanese was very limited, I left them and walked away with as jaunty an air as I could manage.

Later that day, the guard handed over the key to the storeroom where a lot of our personal belongings had been kept since we first came into the camp. The only things I had there were the 24-bass piano accordion that I had brought from Changi, together with my knife and some bits of carved perspex. I took the things back to my room where I tried to play the accordion and was saddened to find that my fingers were far too stiff and, even worse, I couldn't remember any tunes. Later in the day a piano was brought into camp and installed in the mess room, and I found that I couldn't play it either. Then I remembered my collection of papers: notes, sketches and the original slides and script of Robinson Crusoe that, not trusting the Nips' store, I had hidden below the floorboards in my first barrack room. I went back there and the new occupants, all Dutchmen, were very happy to help me to dig them up again. Happily, they all were in fairly good condition, yellowed slightly but otherwise not much the worse for their two and a half years under the building.

The Japanese had promised more food, including meat, but all that I saw come into camp was a small quantity of meat which looked remarkably like dog. For the meal that evening the rice bowls were not quite so full and the cooks explained that the stock was almost exhausted, but there was a good bowl of soup with some small pieces of meat in it. Dog it may have been, but the taste was wonderful!

On the 19th a B29 bomber flew over us and dropped a load of leaflets but there was a fairly strong breeze that day and none landed inside the camp. I should have liked to have one as a souvenir but did not have the strength to go out and search. However, at least one was brought in and its contents were publicised. It said that the Imperial Japanese Army had surrendered and that every effort would be made to repatriate the prisoners as quickly as possible, but in the meantime food and other necessities would be supplied by the US Air Force. The first drop would be made the following day at noon. Sure enough, at about midday on the 20th two or three planes flew over and dropped a cargo by parachute, but it all landed in the hills behind the camp and a long way from us. We got nothing from that drop but I heard later that a young Japanese child had been killed, although we were not told how. Lt. Sliew then marked a big circle in the middle of the parade ground, using flour from the cookhouse and added the words: DROP HERE.

The second drop came next day, the 21st, and was aimed at our parade ground, but oh, dear, what a mess! The big planes flew very low over us to identify the dropping zone and then came round again for the actual drop. The cargo consisted of big 72-gallon oil drums welded end to end in pairs or in threes and attached to cargo 'chutes which, I later saw, bore a label stating that they were to be used for loads of up to 112 lb at 100 miles per hour. With a load of at least twelve-hundredweight, with several at nearer to eighteen, and with a speed more like 200 m.p.h., of course things came apart.

None of the huge canisters landed on the parade ground but several of them hit the barrack blocks, crashing through roof and ceiling, upper floor and lower floor, to finish among the foundations. The others landed outside the camp, on the nearby hills and on the coal washings where, until recently, I had been working. With all those massive canisters crashing around the camp, there was an air of panic, with prisoners dashing in all directions. The parachutes, separated from their loads, just folded up and dropped or drifted down, several of them becoming entangled with the overhead power lines. The result was hilarious chaos. Many of the drums which had landed outside the camp, had burst open with the result that the countryside seemed to be running with bully beef and canned peaches, mixed with Herschey chocolate bars, cigarettes, shirts, trousers, – the lot. Meanwhile, the overhead power lines were putting on a marvellous fireworks display.

Several of our fellows were hurt but, mercifully, no one was killed. Someone remarked that it would have been the height of irony to have survived the war, only to be killed by a can of corned beef. Willing hands soon collected all the goodies, and it was clear that there was more than enough for all. Some of the locals tried to get at the drops which landed outside the camp but any who succeeded in picking up a stray can were summarily relieved of it. The locals were later given plenty of stuff, but at that stage none of us felt any sympathy or compassion whatsoever. We had been warned by Dr. Rappard not to overeat but, predictably, one or two did and of course they became very ill. Digestive systems that had for so long been underfed on a minimal diet of little more than plain rice were in no condition to deal with an overdose of rich foods. I had always been a small eater, a great blessing during our days of near-starvation, and I was most careful with the new and plentiful food. Even so, I developed a nagging pain around my heart and went in some anxiety to see Dr. Rappard. He said that certainly I, like most of the others, was far from well and terribly underweight (I then weighed 36 kilos, or 5 stones, 9lb) but so far as he could tell there was nothing wrong with my heart. He thought the pains were nervous indigestion, probably brought on by the recent excitement. He was sorry but he had no medicine to give me. His diagnosis proved correct and I suffered from nervous indigestion for about twenty years after the war, having all the symptoms of an ulcer without actually having one.

Next day, 22nd August 1945, wearing new light khaki trousers and shirt from the American air drop, and my army boots but no hat, with three friends I thumbed a lift in a local truck to Orio railway station, where we got on a train which took us the ten miles to the town of Yahata. The train was full of Japanese when it stopped at Orio, and there were quite a lot of POWs waiting for it. As there was no room at all for us inside, many of us and one or two of the younger Japanese men just climbed onto the outside. I was on the front of the engine with my legs dangling either side of the left-hand buffer. Nobody asked us for a ticket, and that journey, my first away from the prison camp, was a truly memorable one.

The whole of that northern coastal strip from our camp to Moji, the port where we had landed, was and still is mostly industrial. For much of the way the railway line was elevated slightly above the general level so that from the train we had a good view. I could see at least one reason why Japan had capitulated. It was burned out! For as far as I could see, incendiary bombs had devastated the closely packed domestic buildings which, like our barracks, were made mostly of timber. All that was left was a grey-brown sea of burned out pantiles, slightly thinner on the ground where the narrow roads and lanes had been. The only things standing more than a foot above the burnt tiles were concrete water tanks and various bits of iron machinery. Even the factory buildings, mostly of light steel frames and corrugated sheeting, were burned out, battered and rusty.

Then away ahead of us I could see that some buildings were still standing, and as we drew nearer I could see a flag flying above them. Soon I could see that it was a Union Jack. As the train passed by on its elevated track I noticed that the buildings and the fence surrounding that POW camp were very much the same as ours except that the fence was somewhat charred. I wondered why the camp had survived when all around was burned out. It was difficult to believe that the American Air Force had been so precise in the dropping of their incendiary bombs, even supposing that they knew the exact location of the camp. There was no identification on its roof, as there should have been, but then there had not been any on our roofs either until the day after the war ended: a policy consistent with the intention of the U-shaped tunnel. Finally I concluded that the British occupants had known what to do with those incendiary bombs. They probably scooped them up and threw them into someone else's back yard.

We left the train at Yahata and explored the town. We had very little money but we enjoyed just walking around and looking. Surprisingly, in view of warnings given, we found no antagonism and everyone smiled and tried to be friendly. I never heard of any trouble from the ex-prisoners; we were happy in our new freedom and too intrigued with the strange new world around us to remember our earlier much avowed hatred

My knowledge of the Japanese language was very limited, having been picked up entirely by ear and under a great need for secrecy. However, it was better than that of the others, and so I was in demand when we became lost or when anything was wanted. Our main need was for refreshment, but there was little choice of food on sale. We went into a scrupulously clean restaurant and I asked for four bowls of *soba* (noodles) and some water. The day was hot and we were thirsty. The little waitress was very shy and she and her three colleagues did a lot of giggling, but she soon brought us, with a beautiful smile, a lacquer tray bearing four small glasses and a pint-sized jug of water. We filled the glasses twice and needed some more water, but then I had an idea and asked the waitress to bring us four of the jugs. She looked surprised, even horrified, but then brought the four jugs and we amused the other occupants of the place by drinking directly from them. After all, they were just about the same as a pint tankard. That broke the ice for us and soon we were passing American cigarettes around among the other customers. 'Are you Americans?' they wanted to know. 'No, we're English', I replied and they looked surprised. Presumably they were expecting American occupation forces, and we were wearing American clothes. 'We were prisoners of war', I added in explanation. 'Aah! Is that so?', and they all bowed to us, suddenly looking very embarrassed.

The fact that we were extremely emaciated would not have been very noticeable to those Japanese men and women because they were too. We enjoyed their discomfort for a brief moment but soon the cigarettes were out again and there was a not very successful attempt at conversation before we went on our wandering way, followed by sincere calls of '*Sayonara!*' It was a most interesting first meeting with the ordinary people and a day I shall always remember. We all managed to find seats in the train back to Orio, and got a lift back to camp. While we were waiting for a lift, another train came in from the same direction and its engine was covered with ex-POWs. That little sortie had taken a lot out of me because, after all, I was still a bag of bones and my legs were aching, and so I spent the whole of the next day just resting. On the 24th we had our third air drop, but this time we were much better prepared for it. Somehow, Lt. Sliew had got a message through to the US Air Force to ask for the drop to be on the large area of coal washings outside the camp and everyone was ready for it.

All those who were fit enough to do so stripped down to a pair of boots and a loin cloth and, armed with any digging implements we could find, together with some lengths of rope, we sat and waited for the arrival of the planes. As soon as we heard them we dashed out and formed a ring around the large black area, and when the bombers flew over on their first run we all waved at them. The bomb bays were open and we could see the fliers inside and waving back. Then we all ran away from the danger area and waited for their return. I was on the roadway which ran in front of the camp and across the end of the coal mud area, with houses on the far side. By the time the bombers returned, several of the inhabitants had come out to watch the fun, and I was intrigued by the comments of some of those who were standing beside me.

'*Okii! Taihen okii*' (Big! Very big!) Their words and gasps were all of surprise and wonderment because they had never before seen planes so big but, come to that, neither had I. This time the drop was remarkably successful and every one of the big canisters landed in the coal dust mud. Even so, many of the 'chutes were torn lose and once again they tangled with the power lines and house tops. We all dashed onto the mud to dig out the drums, none of which were damaged although some were about twelve feet down in the soft ground. While we were digging and pushing and pulling, the planes came round again for a third run, this time to make a more personal drop. Out of the bomb bays came dozens of small bundles of newspapers and magazines, many of them bearing scrawled short messages of good wishes and the words: 'See you in Okinawa'. They also dropped several of the big reels of aluminium foil tape that were intended to be chopped up into short lengths and dropped from a great height as 'window' to mislead the enemy's radar. That aluminium foil unrolled as it fell and much of it landed across the power lines, causing even more fireworks displays

The general effect of all this upon the Japanese was shattering. For years they had been fed on propaganda to the effect that they were winning the war, while America was starving, Britain was starving, and there was no meat in Australia. Now all kinds of goodies were raining down by the ton, while aluminium, not seen in Japan for many long years, was actually being thrown away.

It was at about this time that we received a warning that under no circumstances should we go to Nagasaki, about a hundred miles away to the south west as the crow flies but a hundred and forty miles by train. No one knew precisely why but we gathered that a new kind of bomb had been dropped there and it had left something electric in the soil. How else could they explain to us about radiation?

Saturday, 25th August was spent in camp, resting. There was also talk of a concert and so once again I tried to play my accordion but without success. My fingers were far too stiff, and I still couldn't think of any tunes. This was a little worrying because all my life I have carried a tune with me; any tune would do, either whistling or humming the melody. A Dutchman asked if he might borrow the accordion and I was delighted to lend it

We decided to erect flags at our gateway and this led to some interesting planning, the leader amongst the British being Sergeant Bill Sharp. Mild and gently spoken, he had had the great misfortune to lose all four fingers of one hand in an accident down the pit. Bill's leadership and determination in the matter of putting up a Union Flag were a great credit to him, and a fine example to us all. Several of us spent most of Sunday morning collecting coloured parachutes: red, white and blue, but then we discovered that there was only one sewing machine and the American party had got to it first. This was a potential setback, but it did not daunt Bill Sharp.

He scrounged some thread and an assortment of needles, some of which had been made in Changi from sardine can keys. He found a big pair of scissors, and under his unflagging leadership several of us spent all of Sunday afternoon and all of that night busily sewing a huge Union Flag by hand. Someone, I don't remember who, remarked with typical pragmatic philosophy, that while the Union Flag was complicated enough, he was glad that we did not have to sew the Stars and Stripes by hand, and perhaps the Yanks had the greater need of the machine. In my imagination I can still see that sewing party, and Bill using his maimed hand with obvious skill.

Meanwhile others had been scrounging around the neighbourhood and had found two tall flag poles, one for each side of the gateway. On Monday morning, after a breakfast still of rice but with a reasonable portion of bully beef, and a cup of real tea, I lent a hand with the erection of the two masts: one for the Union Flag and the other for 'Old Glory'. Then in the afternoon we had a 'flags up' ceremony outside on the roadway. Every American, British and Australian ex-prisoner who was able to walk was on parade, all wearing new US Army drill shirts and slacks and looking as smart as we could. The parade was hardly up to Brigade of Guards standards, but it showed to any onlooker that the recently downtrodden ex-prisoners were by no means cowed and had plenty of spirit and discipline left. The point was not wasted on the crowd of Japanese locals who stood behind us. There was, however, a rather sad aspect to the 'flags up' ceremony in that it excluded the Dutch who greatly outnumbered the British, Australians and Americans put together. They had to be content with a flagstaff at the far end of the parade ground, and they studiously ignored our ceremony as, later, we ignored theirs. On the 28th August there was another food drop, the second on the coal mud, and it brought an almost exact repeat of all the fun of four days earlier. I took my turn with a spade and the rope and then spent the day just sitting and talking.

An Australian sergeant (at least that is the rank he claimed) raised the question of what was to be done with the ashes of our dead. I cannot be certain of the exact numbers, but I think we lost six Australians, ten or twelve British, and about thirty Dutch. There were no deaths among the sixty or seventy Americans in the camp. The ashes of each, or at least all that were collected after the cremations, were in boxes made of thin, untreated pine and about six-inch cubes. That sounds quite small but in fact those little boxes, labelled only with the Japanese characters for the prison numbers, were surprisingly heavy, each weighing a little less than six kilos, or about thirteen pounds.

Not wanting to leave any of them in Japan, it was quickly decided that we should take all back to their countries of origin, and then it seemed to be best to have a crate for each of the three groups. I made a few measurements and then, deciding that the Dutchmen had better have two crates, I undertook to get them made. Accompanied by the Australian sergeant, I walked across the village to the house of Lt. Suematsu, which I had visited on one previous occasion while out looking for rabbit food. I marched in, boots and all, (and to hell with his tatami matted floors!) and after saluting smartly - but *not* bowing - told him what we wanted. At first he protested a bit and seemed to be surprised that we should want to take all of the ash when, apparently, he thought that a 'representative sample' would be sufficient, but I insisted and repeated: '*Hai. Zembun*!' (Yes. All!) It was then that he suddenly sat up straight and his mouth and eyes opened wide. He had just recognised Megane Baka, the bespectacled fool. The conversation, all in very stilted Japanese, continued for a short time and I received a polite promise to have the crates made and delivered within three days, as requested. The delivery was duly made and the little boxes were crated up. The Australian sergeant volunteered to escort one case back to Australia, the two big ones for the Dutch were handed to Lt. Sliew, and I think it was Bill Sharp who took charge of the British crate.

I went alone to Kokura on the 2nd September, just to look around the town, and while there I made a rough sketch of a gateway to a shrine near the old and rather decrepit castle. An elderly Japanese man wearing clean, cream-coloured *koku min fuku* (national dress) came up to me and in tolerably good English gave me an historical account of the castle but, sadly, I did not take notes and all too quickly forgot the details. That evening, back in camp, I heard that Lt. Suematsu was giving a small party for all the officers in the camp (another insurance premium?), and, later, that each of them received a paper model of an ancient samurai warrior's helmet, packed in a cardboard box of about the same size as those containing the ashes.

The Aussie sergeant mentioned earlier was a real 'bluffer' who was generally believed to have promoted himself, and immediately *he* wanted one of those helmets. Doubtless he was going to tell the tale when he got home and, who knows, he might get a commission out of it! He asked if I could help him to buy one. I cared nothing for his morals, or what he wanted to do with his gift, but was quite happy to have such a challenge. The next day, the 3rd September, three Australians and I went to Kokura and to a big department store I had noticed on the previous day. While the three 'diggers' stood and listened, I quizzed a succession of young lady assistants, each of whom said she understood but then burst into giggles and ran away, to return in a moment or two with another assistant. This went on for some time until one young woman suddenly said that she really did understand. She said some magic words which I didn't understand, away went one of the giggling girls and in a moment or two the model helmet, identical in every way to those presented by Suematsu, was produced. The Aussie paid for it, I thanked the assembled young ladies, who bowed to me - we bowed - they bowed - we bowed - and then finally went away. I quite enjoyed that linguistic foray, but goodness knows what they thought of my Japanese, which was not only grammatically incorrect, but was also in the sometimes quite vulgar vernacular of the mine. It was to be several years before I learned a modicum of politeness.

Our fifth food drop was on the 4th September and as before I stripped off to boots and a loin cloth and helped to dig it out. When I got back to camp I saw that a stray parachute had tangled with our flagstaff at the gate and had broken it off. Everyone wanted to have the flag back up again as quickly as possible, but the pole was broken beyond repair and we needed a new one. It was then that I recalled seeing a tall flagstaff when I was out foraging for dandelions for those bloody rabbits.

It had been in a little courtyard about half a mile to the west so I gathered three friends, who found two adjustable spanners and a very blunt saw, and next morning we set off, finding the mast more or less as remembered. The buildings appeared to be fairly new and some sort of shrine complex, with the mast in the middle of a small open square, but as soon as we got to it we could see problems.

Instead of being in a proper tabernacle, within which it could pivot and be lowered to the ground, this one was just bolted to a single concrete post - and the bolts were completely rusted up. The only way was to saw it off. Unfortunately, the only place where the mast could be dropped was at one corner of the square, the way we had walked in, where there was a gap of about ten feet between the corners of the buildings.

A notch was cut in the mast above the concrete (a pity to lose four feet but it could not be avoided) on the side nearest to the gap and then we started to saw on the far side. Eventually, with the others sawing in turns, I stood on top of the post and pushed the mast towards the gap. All went well until the crucial moment, when there was a puff of wind and in spite of my puny efforts the mast swung to the left and well over the corner of a building. I was quite sure that all our efforts were wasted and that the mast would break itself on the solid looking roof, but then came the surprise. It went down like a hot knife through butter, through the tiled roof, through the ceiling and the two adjacent side walls, to land unbroken on the ground, leaving a triangular piece of the building standing in odd looking isolation. When first seen, the building had appeared to be strong and sturdy but it was now seen as being of the lightest of timber sections and a lot of paper. With a little cheer we pulled the mast clear, picked up our trophy and carried it triumphantly back to camp, where it was erected next day without ceremony.

Towards evening on Saturday, the 8th September, four rather strange looking orientals walked into the camp. They spoke no English and only a word or two of Japanese but eventually it was discovered, I'm not sure how, that they were Chinese and had been prisoners for a long time. They were dressed in rags but yet did not appear to be as emaciated as we were. They were shown to the mess room and invited to bed down there, which they did with alacrity. Needless to say, there was plenty of food for them, including some freshly cooked rice, and I think they were given some American clothing. Goodness knows, they needed it! My personal recollection of the four is that their ever-present grins rivalled those of the Gurkhas.

At 11 a.m. on Thursday, 13th September 1945, just over four weeks after the war ended, two Americans walked into the camp. I have seen some big men but those two were giants. Both appeared to be of Italian stock, with rather swarthy complexions and heads covered with short but thick black curls. Each was like a walking arsenal, being hung around with automatic rifles, two enormous automatic pistols in holsters, and with grenades and ammo clips dangling from their belts. After a quick talk with the officers on the parade ground, one of the visitors departed but the other was taken to the mess hall and given coffee and biscuits. I asked to see one of his pistols, which almost disappeared in his big fist, but when he handed it to me I nearly dropped it, it was so heavy.

Apparently he and his colleague were paratroopers, only two of a large number whose duty, if an invasion of Japan had come, would have been to drop as closely as possible to all the known POW camps. The aim was to reach and to arm a few of the fitter prisoners, and to 'hold the fort' until relief forces could reach them overland. When capitulation came, as the direct result of two special bombs which he called 'atom bombs', the bulk of the airborne force was not needed, but a few had landed and were going from camp to camp just to see that all was well. When reassured that we were indeed all right and just waiting to be taken home, having finished his coffee he walked out of the camp and on his way.

After our paratrooper friend had gone I went to collect three friends with whom, it had been agreed, we should visit Shimonoseki. When the four of us arrived at the gate we saw that some Dutchmen were setting up a table and some chairs on the verandah of the guardroom while others were marshalling about forty Japanese men into line on the parade ground. A second look showed that they were all the section chiefs, and I recognised several, including the Pig. Having nothing to do with the exercise but curious about it, the four of us stood for a while to watch the proceedings.

Quickly each Nip was brought up to the table and quizzed by three Dutchmen, none of them officers, but I could not hear what was said, nor even the language used. Eventually they had all been separated into two groups, presumed by me to be 'sheep' and 'goats'.

Then two tall Dutchmen went to one of the groups and proceeded to give two clouts to each, after the manner of the Nips. However, the difference was that in this case the smiter was much taller than the smitten. 'Those must be the bad ones,' I observed, and expected to see the others being dismissed, but at that moment the big gates were opened wide and in came a horse and cart. In fact it was the 'honey cart', very long and narrow, barely thirty inches wide, and on it were two rows of wooden tubs, each about a foot wide and about three feet tall, normally used to cart away the sludge from the tanks under our toilets.

The foul-smelling mess was ladled up in long handled wooden pots and the tubs were then fitted with a big wooden stopper before being lifted onto the cart and taken away to the fields to be used as a fertiliser. That work was normally done by the lowest caste of Japanese, once called 'eta', but on that Thursday the job was done differently.

It was the Nips who had been beaten who were escorted to the gate while the others, including the Pig, were each told to take a tub and to fill it from the nearest benjo (literally, 'shit house'). They were not given a bung but were then told to carry the full tub up the hill at the back of the camp and to bring it down again. Well, it doesn't take much imagination to picture the result. Each of those Nips finished the course covered all over from head to foot with 'sweet vi-o-lets' as the old song says. All the British and Australians in the camp were disgusted and some protested but the Dutchmen were adamant, saying that it was the only kind of treatment likely to be really understood. My friends and I, too weak both physically and morally to intervene, went on our way to Shimonoseki.

Some thirty-nine years later I was asked about that incident. Not only the participants but also their families and friends knew of the treatment, considering it to have been utterly degrading and an unwarranted insult. What did I think of it? I replied that I had disapproved when I saw it, but at the same time had felt that we had suffered much at the hands of the Japanese. Perhaps those particular Japanese, our erstwhile section leaders, had not been the worst but they were the only ones to hand and, like it or not, they had to stand as *daihyo* (representative) for their nation.

The honey cart incident expressed our need for revenge in a way which really got through to the Japanese. They had always been so arrogant but also so compulsively clean, but yet, unlike most of the treatment we had received from them, it left no more permanent a scar than could be removed by a good bath. If there was still a lingering smell in their nostrils, well, I could still smell Singapore.

During the night of 16th September a typhoon hit the north coast of Kyushu, causing a lot of damage. When we emerged at first light on the 17th we found that most of the barrack blocks had lost tiles, particularly those which had been 'bombed' during the food drops. However, the greatest damage was to the large mess room, which was now flattened except for the kitchens on the eastern end.

We were surveying the damage when someone remembered that our four Chinese friends had been sleeping in the hall. Many willing hands dragged the damaged sheets of roof construction away, and found the Chinese below. They emerged from the debris, apparently quite unhurt and still grinning.

Another phenomenon of the storm was that a heavy wooden sentry box which had stood in the corner of the fence by the kitchen was now not to be seen. Then it was spotted some two hundred or more feet up the mountain at the back of the camp. Several stretches of the high boundary fence were down, but that was now of no interest to anybody.

CHAPTER NINE

JOURNEY HOME

The British and Australian prisoners, together with the slightly smaller American party, were warned to be ready to leave camp at 5.30 a.m. on Tuesday, 18th September, 1945. However, as with most things in those days, nothing was ever quite as good as promised. In fact we left at 9.30 a.m. and were loaded, clutching our poor belongings, into a line of cattle trucks which had stopped outside the camp gate. 'Aye, aye!' someone remarked. 'In the shit to the very last!' Those trucks were not very clean but, mercifully, we were in them for only a short time before we were out again and standing on the platform at Orio Station. A train of carriages with separate compartments, not as luxurious as those in which we had arrived two and a half years previously, but yet quite comfortable and very clean, stopped at the platform soon after the cattle trucks had departed. In a very leisurely way, it was intimated that we should climb aboard.

I noticed Lt. Suematsu standing at one end of the platform and rather tentatively offering to shake hands but he was getting very few takers and certainly I wanted no more to do with him. As the train drew out he was to be seen standing rather forlornly as a solitary figure, still at the end of the platform. Although I did not know it at the time, he was the last Japanese I was to see for twenty-four years.

Never having seen anything of the country other than that in the immediate vicinity of our camp, and on our recent trips along that coast as far as Moji, I was delighted to travel in daylight. Between the making of that journey and the typing up of these notes many years have elapsed and I have been back to Japan and to

Kyushu four times, and three times back to the village, now grown to a town, of Mizumaki-cho, the location of the mine. The result is that some of the remembered pictures have become rather mixed up. However, of that 140-mile railway journey there are still some very clear memories. At various places after passing through Fukuoka the line ran close to the sea, and from my window on the right-hand side I could see small fishing villages dotted along the coast. Almost without exception they had badly damaged buildings, torn to pieces by the recent typhoon. It seemed almost as if the storm had been in league with the 'dragon-slaying' atom bombs, not to mention the countless incendiary ones, to wreak vengeance and swift retribution on the whole country. It was a comforting thought, soon to be echoed in one way or another by remarks from my companions in the compartment. But then, as the journey proceeded, the visible damage became more widespread, almost total, and once again the spoken comments echoed my own quite spontaneous thoughts: 'You poor little buggers!' However, having accepted that thought of compassion, I hastily pushed it to the back of my mind and tried to contemplate the passing scene with complete detachment. I remember thinking how picturesque those little villages must have been, and wishing that I could have had the opportunity to sketch. The main attraction was that they appeared to be completely rural and a relic of the Old Japan. I have visited some of those villages in comparatively recent days but they are no longer picturesque, being over-full of red and white signs with meanings more or less equal to 'Eat at Joe's'.

Suddenly, and with little warning, we came to the area where the world's second atomic bomb had exploded. The memory is of travelling along a stretch of lowland, perhaps a mile wide and flanked on both sides by lines of hills, perhaps 1500 feet high. That valley through which the train moved at a snail's pace would have been five or six miles long, and all one could see throughout its length and breadth, even up the hill sides in the distance, was complete desolation.

In some respects the scene was very similar to that already described along the north coast of Kyushu, around Yahata, Kokura and Moji with greyish coloured burned-out roofing tiles, through which projected the numerous concrete water tubs and cast iron mangles. But our attention was soon attracted to the heavier structures which, in the most spectacular way, demonstrated the power of the atom bomb. Heavy steel-framed structures had been bent into strange shapes; reinforced concrete buildings were crushed and shattered and had large pieces hanging off at unusual angles. A weird effect which particularly caught my eye was a large reinforced concrete chimney which had had its top fused and bent over, reminiscent of a ship's ventilator pipe. My thought at the time was that much of the scene reminded me of a bramble bush on a heath in wintertime.

It took us about three quarters of an hour to pass through that terrible place in which not a living soul was to be seen, and we in our compartment were dashing from side to side of the carriage in response to the excited calls: 'Gosh! Just look at this!' At that time we knew nothing at all about radiation and its horrible effects, and of course we saw no evidence of it. What we did see was much akin to the damage caused by the more usual high explosives or with incendiaries, except that it was so obviously many times more extensive, much more powerful, and accompanied by great heat.

As the train crawled along the valley, between periods of amazement at the sights, I was aware of a mental process of balancing my thoughts and emotions; of equating satisfaction on the basis of an eye for an eye with compassion for the countless 'ordinary folk'. I then remembered some of the things I had seen: the strung together corpses of those women and children on the beach at Changi, those who had been raped after death in the streets of Singapore, the cinema films I had seen of the attack on Nanking, the many comrades who had died of starvation and disease, and that U-shaped tunnel above the camp that, in the event of invasion, would have been our unmarked grave.

Then I thought of the ordinary inhabitants of Nagasaki, those men and women now dead who were probably much the same as some of the kindly folk with whom I had talked in Yahata and Kokura. But yet they were also of the same people who would quite cheerfully have immured me and my friends in that tunnel and, with stony faces and reptilian eyes, denied that we had ever been there. Clearly they were all so much indoctrinated that there was no other way. No, horrible though it was, I for one felt grateful for that atom bomb, and it is only fair to say that, so many years later, I am still of the same mind. My present concern is that the Japanese nation, or at least its government, has done another 'tunnel job' and has tried to suppress and conceal from its later generations the truth about what was done in the name of the emperor.

I don't remember passing through Nagasaki station. Probably it had been blown away by the bomb. Eventually the train stopped at a long platform some twenty feet above a quay where I could see the grey paint of naval vessels tied up alongside. We all scrambled out with our personal belongings. I had a big pack on my back and my small piano accordion without a case slung over my shoulder. There was a brass band playing somewhere. We turned left along the platform, shepherded by a few American servicemen, who were patting backs and shaking hands as we moved to the end of the long platform.

Coming to its end, I could see that a barrier was made of trestle tables covered with white cloths, and behind the table were standing three or four WHITE WOMEN!! The capital letters indicate the effect on me, and those around me, of those ladies. To be strictly honest, none of them were really pretty; in fact they were a rather tough-looking lot but yet to us, ex-prisoners who had not seen a white woman for three and a half years, they looked absolutely wonderful. I approached the table shyly and one of the white-coated goddesses put a paper cup of very hot coffee into my right hand. 'Here! Take this. Glad to see you, fella!', and I was nudged to the left to the next goddess who greeted me.

'Hi, fella! Glad to see you! Stick out your hand!' I held out my left hand, palm upwards. 'Open your fingers!', and she stuck three hot and very sugary doughnuts over my extended digits. Now what to do? We were being nudged gently but inexorably along towards a building some fifty yards away; the coffee was far too hot to drink and the only way to attack the doughnuts was to hold up the left hand and nibble. By the time I reached the building I had a burned tongue, a paper cup still three quarters full of near-boiling coffee, a sticky doughnut on my middle finger, and sugar all over my face! I felt very guilty about the unnecessary waste when I dumped the coffee and the one remaining doughnut and went into the building.

Immediately inside was a line of tables where American sailors in white overalls took all our gear, with the promise that it would be returned unharmed later, after it had been de-loused. My big pack was tagged, as was a large canvas bag into which they put my accordion, then both were pumped full of a white powder. I asked what it was and was told the then meaningless letters DDT, to kill all the bugs and lice. I replied with feeling that I wished we had had some of that magic powder some two and a half years ago.

Next I had to remove every stitch of clothing and, although they were no more than a month old and in excellent condition, they all were hastily bundled into big paper bags and sent to the incinerator. I was then ushered, completely naked through a double-door airlock into a room full of steam which, of course, condensed on my battered spectacles. I was grasped by two very sturdy and equally naked Americans who guided, not to say pushed, me under a triple shower where they soaped and scrubbed me all over. I had to put my feet one at a time on a block and while one sailor steadied me the other scrubbed with a special thin brush between all the toes. The same treatment was given to the hands and then great attention was given to the navel, under the armpits and in the crotch. That process took nearly twenty minutes, after which I was patted gently on the bum, told I was 'done', and directed through another double door to a drying room. There, two more men towelled me dry and directed me round a corner and in to the next 'room' of what must have been a very long corridor, doubling back on itself so as to fit compactly into the one building. I turned the corner and was pounced upon by several men at once. They were all in white, wore gas masks, and were armed with huge metal syringes which emitted powerful jets of DDT powder. Like any well cosseted infant, I was powdered all over, again with particular attention to toes, navel and crotch

I turned another corner and into a broad corridor with three or four table-high couches down its centre line, each couch being presided over by a white gowned and masked doctor. They checked that all limbs were intact and working, listened to the chest, and prodded and pummelled all over the body. Finally I was told: 'You'll do. Good luck, sonny!' and sent walking on my naked way around the next corner. Some of my comrades obviously would not 'do', those who had lost limbs or were too weak being directed to a hospital ship, but I don't know how they got aboard.

My next stop was at a long counter where I was handed two vests, two pairs of pants, a pair of rubber-soled leather boots (which I wore for many years later on geological field trips), a pair of khaki drill trousers and a dark green windproof jacket with large patch-pockets. There was no shirt and no socks. I also received a large cloth kit bag. Dressing myself in the new clothes, all of which hung baggily on my scraggy frame, at the end of the long corridor I collected my accordion and big pack and moved out of the building.

I was standing on a small landing at the top of a wooden stair which led down some twenty feet to a quayside. To the right was a high brick retaining wall while on the left was the grey painted side of the hospital ship. Beyond it could be seen a smaller naval vessel, later identified as the US Destroyer 'Wadsworth'. All the quay was full of ex-prisoners, with a few US servicemen mixed among them. They were all chatting quietly but the sum of their voices was a gentle though all-pervading roar. At the bottom of the steps were more tables, presided over by more American ladies, this time somewhat older and wearing dark blue uniforms of the Red Cross. There I was given another cup of coffee, but I politely declined the doughnuts. Those ladies also gave me a small draw-string bag of 'comforts' which included a tooth brush and paste, nail brush, soap in a plastic box, a comb and small mirror, a writing pad and envelopes, a pencil, a packet of twenty 'Camel' cigarettes and a book of matches.

I moved through the crowd to the wall at the back, set down my gear, lit a cigarette and studied the scene. I knew most of the ex-POWs, at least by sight, but yet somehow their faces were different. Of course all were still emaciated but yet the once drawn and unsmiling faces were all lit by a new vivacity. I had stood there for only about five minutes when a young American naval lieutenant came up to me and without any introduction started to chat. I never knew his name or his job but he was full of curiosity about my immediate past history, my pre-war job and my hopes for the future when I returned home. Needless to say, I was more than eager to talk and we had been chatting for some time when another lieutenant came up, nodded briefly to my new friend and asked me: 'Sir. I'm sorry to interrupt but would you like to join my ship? I should like to sail.' Looking around, I was embarrassed to see that the quay was empty and I was the last ex-POW there. The lieutenant led the way along the quay, carrying my accordion, and cheerfully repeated some of the many questions asked by his colleague. We eventually went aboard the destroyer where I found several dozen of my fellow ex-POWs. The lieutenant excused himself politely and went away, and within a few minutes we were moving out into the Nagasaki waterway. The time would have been about 4 p.m. on Tuesday, 18th September, 1945. At last I had left Japan.

The first thing I noticed about the USS Wadswoth was the almost overwhelming friendliness of the crew. I never knew how many ex-POWs were on board but would guess at least fifty, maybe more. We were scattered all over the upper deck and well mixed with the crew, all of whom were most solicitous for our comfort. The ship moved out into Nagasaki roads and then dropped anchor, apparently waiting for another vessel to join us. At about 5 p.m. there was a call to the mess room and we were escorted by our hosts to a quickly moving queue and then to a serving counter where a line of cooks were cheerfully doling out the 'goodies'. One very large negro clucked over us like a mother hen, urging us to accept more food on the grounds that we: 'looked as if we needed to be fattened up some'. I was glad of that food, and then realised that, apart from two sugary doughnuts and a cup of coffee, I had not eaten since a rather scrappy breakfast more than twelve hours ago. Still, I declined the kindly negro's offers and accepted only a very moderate helping of...everything that was going.

We were intrigued by the way the food was served directly onto stainless steel trays into which several dents had been pressed. The advantages of this over the swill bucket method we had met on the Strathmore and the Ekma were immediately apparent. Also, and even allowing for our eagerness as ex-POWs, the quality of the food was much higher than I had ever experienced in the British Army. The loaded tray was then carried to any vacant place at one of several mess tables, on each of which there was a jug of milk, salt and pepper, and a big bowl of *sugar*! 'Hey! Look at that! I haven't seen that much sugar since I came to Japan!' I quickly put two teaspoonfuls into my mug of tea and stirred well, but the tea still did not taste sweet. In the end I had the equivalent of two heaped dessert spoons before that mug of tea was sweet. The condition lasted for several days until my palate was once more able to appreciate sugar, when I returned to a modest one teaspoonful.

When darkness came, a cinema screen was erected on deck and we saw a film: Edward G. Robinson in *Mr Winkle Goes to War*. Over the next few weeks I must have seen more than forty films but that is the only title I can remember.

It was then bed time and all the ex-POWs were led below and shown our sleeping places: bunk beds consisting of V-spring mattresses with a flock overlay, suspended three high on tubular steel frames and vastly better than hammocks. I asked how it was that the ship could have so many free beds and was told that the crew had given up their own cots to us while they slept 'hard' on the open deck. After a quick shower I turned in on a middle level bunk and had the best night's sleep in years. There were no bugs in that bed, I knew there were no bugs, it was beautifully comfortable and those crisp white sheets smelt delightful.

Next morning, Wednesday, 19th September, we sailed away from Nagasaki behind a cruiser, the USS Biloxi, heading for Okinawa, about four hundred miles away. However, after about an hour we hove to while the Biloxi sailed on. Apparently the lookout had spotted a mine bobbing about on the surface about a hundred and fifty yards away to our starboard. Suddenly and without any warning, 'World War III' started as every gun on that side of the ship opened up. All those with belted ammunition had the fifth round as a 'tracer' and so we could see the enormous cascade of shot as it all impinged upon the mine. I was expecting to see a great and spectacular water-spout but none came, and after about fifteen minutes of frenzied attack, all firing ceased and the mine was assumed to have been sunk. Two hours later another mine was spotted, and we did it all again.

After another film show we spent a second night in our borrowed beds and then, at about 1.30 p.m. on the 20th, we dropped anchor not far from the Biloxi in a large bay which appeared to be crammed full of hundreds of naval vessels of all shapes and sizes.

The afternoon passed uneventfully, except that a young crewman came to ask if I would sell him my accordion. In fact I had very little use for it and should have liked to be rid of it, but then suddenly I felt guilty. It was not really mine to sell. I had been given it as a means of entertaining such prisoners as might be my companions. I refused to sell, to the great disappointment of the young sailor, but later, after we had landed I met a US padre and gave it to him. Ever since then I have wished that I had given it to that young sailor. Ah, well.

We were then told that reveille next day would be at 2.30 a.m. because we were to be transferred to the Biloxi at 4 a.m. and taken round the Island to Naha, where we would go ashore. After the early reveille in the dark, and a quick breakfast, we sat on deck in the light of a full moon and just waited. I recall sitting with Jim Hope, an elderly Australian who had been a rubber planter somewhere in Malaya. He found sitting rather painful, having had a groove taken out of both buttocks by a stray bullet which caught him sideways. After the war he sent food parcels from Australia to myself and others who had been his friends in the camp. While Jim and I were sitting on deck we saw an unusual event: a brilliant and spectacular lunar rainbow, the first I had seen. The brief shower which provided the rainbow had passed very quickly so that above us once again there was a velvety black sky sprinkled with brilliantly twinkling stars, while across the bay were the countless riding lights and others of the large fleet of ships. Above, and against a completely black area of sky, there suddenly appeared the rainbow in a complete arch of surprisingly bright colours.

The rainbow had barely faded when a landing craft pulled alongside and without delay we all climbed down into it. Surprisingly quickly and without ceremony we were on our way to the Biloxi. Now, I boast of being a reasonably good sailor, having been in a variety of rough weather in a wide assortment of craft without ever feeling sick. I was not sick on that short trip but must admit to feeling extremely apprehensive and uncomfortable. The craft was like a floating box, about eight feet deep so that we, standing up and swaying about as the vessel chugged through a choppy sea, could see nothing but the night sky above us. The freeboard must have been only a couple of feet or so because at frequent intervals waves broke over the side and drenched us. I thought of how unpleasant it must have been to be put ashore in one of those craft in battle conditions. I was very glad when, without warning, we bumped alongside the Biloxi and rope ladders were lowered. We stayed on deck for the next couple of hours or so while the Biloxi sailed about thirty miles round the island to Naha, and eventually were put ashore at a recently constructed pier of rough coral.

Very soon after being landed we were picked up by a fleet of trucks and jeeps and taken a mile or two to a camp which I hardly remember although we were there for three days. We saw only a small part of the island, that at the southern end around Naha and the airstrip, but my memories are of a land all dusty and yellow, completely devoid of vegetation. How much of that denudation was due to battle and how much was the work of the subsequent construction gangs I could not tell, but it all looked very strange and not at all like the sub-tropical Island I had expected. All the ex-POWs in my company were worried by the American drivers, who dashed around at breakneck speed...on the wrong side of the road! It was my first experience of driving on the right and quite unnerving.

Next morning there was a 4.30 reveille and at about 6 a.m., some Dutchmen were taken to the airstrip and did not return. I went with another party, all British I think, but only one plane load of twenty got away. We were then told that there were no other planes fit to fly and we were taken back to camp. Nothing at all happened on the next day, Sunday, and we all were rather edgy, but I was feeling very tired and slept for most of that day.

On Monday, 22nd September 1945, after another 4.30 a.m. reveille and a snack breakfast, we went at 6.30 a.m. to the airfield and at 8.30 a.m. I left with nineteen others, all strangers to me, in a B24 bomber. For many years I had been fascinated by aeroplanes and flying but hitherto had never had the opportunity to even go aboard a plane, let alone to fly in one This looked like being my first opportunity, but I had heard that we were being carried in the bomb bays, seated on inserted wooden benches. I had no objection to that in itself but it was clear that while so seated I should not be able to see anything at all of the take-off and flight and so would miss a novel experience. When the time came to climb aboard I hung back a little and struck up a conversation with a young flying officer who was standing nearby. In doing so, my back was turned to the plane so that when the other men had climbed aboard, it was he who suggested that we had better continue our conversation aboard. He helped me up the steps and we moved across a completely empty cabin and leant on the far wall, on either side of a window.

A moment or two later, a large young man in a flying suit climbed aboard, saw to the closing of the door and then, in a loud and authoritative voice, addressed his passengers. I cannot remember all he said, only his concluding words, which were: '...and I want no smoking in the bomb bay!' The pilot went up to his flight deck and, seconds later, the four engines were roaring and we were moving. I watched from the window, so fascinated that all thoughts of conversation were suspended. The ground whizzed past, faster and faster, and then abruptly it slowed down and fell away. We were flying!

That flight of some seven hundred miles over the Phillipines Sea to North Luzon lasted about two and a half hours and, except for when the pilot spotted some red and yellow wreckage and spiralled down for a closer look, it was uneventful and rather boring. It was also very tiring because, although we were able to smoke, there was nowhere to sit down. However, the conversation proceeded very happily.

My friend explained that he was 'gunnery crew' and now was out of a job, little more than a passenger although he had to stay with his plane. Then he said: 'I suppose you older men think us awful kids flying these kites!' 'Older men?', I protested. 'How old do you think I am? I'm only twenty-six.' 'Ah,' said my friend, 'I'm only twenty - and the pilot's nineteen!' I forget that young man's name but do recall that he was a trainee accountant, like my brother.

We landed at about 12.30 p.m. at a semi-deserted airfield called, I think, Clarke Field, in the north of Luzon. We had thought we were going to Manila but for some unexplained reason here we were, perhaps a hundred of us, like lost sheep. We were told that another plane would arrive soon to take us on to Manila but nothing happened. We sat on our kitbags at the side of the runway until about 2 p.m., when we were walked to a mess room and given some tea and biscuits. After which we walked back and just hung about, but there was not a moving plane of any kind to be seen. Some of us were becoming a little tetchy, not to say hungry, but then at about 5 p.m. we were collected in an assortment of trucks, driven back to the camp area and shown to some large pyramid-shaped tents, each of which contained about twenty beds on wooden floors. A short time later we were called and walked to the mess for a much needed evening meal.

That was fine until it was discovered that we did not have any mess tins and the canteen did not have any plates or pressed steel trays. Out we went again, back to the tents, and I could hear a lot of rather bad-tempered muttering, but within half an hour we were summoned again. As we filed into the quite large mess hall I saw another line of men in various stages of undress coming into the hall from the opposite side. I recall thinking: 'Now we shall have to wait until these more legitimate users get their meal. A pity we had to hang around for so long. I'm famished.'

Our queue made straight for the serving counter and the other line curled around, apparently making for the same spot. But as it approached ours, meeting at the start of the serving counter, each American handed over his mess tins and knife, fork and spoon to an ex-POW, my counterpart saying to me: 'My name's Block, Hut 34. Enjoy your meal and I'll see you later.'

I did enjoy my meal and then, after carefully washing the mess tins and cutlery, I sought out Tent No. 34 and rather shyly asked for Mr Block. 'Sure, Buddy. Come on in! Meet my friend Winston Hanson', and the two flyers then entertained me for the rest of the evening, some four hours until midnight, on rum and coke. As usual, cigarettes were passed but when I produced a book of matches Block insisted that I should accept a lighter, saying that he had several. I used that lighter all the way home and for several years after. I still have it although it is not used now.

Next morning at 10 a.m. we took off again, this time sitting on the floor in a large transport plane which took us some 250 miles south to Nicholls Field, Manila. From there we were taken by truck to an extensive transit camp of pyramidal tents, run by the Australian Army for the sole purpose of re-patriating ex-prisoners of war.

I was in that transit camp for twenty-two days and did very little other than eat, sleep and put on weight. We were woken for breakfast, midday and evening meals, and there was no limit on the food. Breakfast, for example, offered cornflakes or porridge, or both if you wished, followed by bacon, eggs, tomatoes and fried bread, followed again by toast, butter and marmalade, jam or honey.

And if one helping was insufficient, well, you just took your empty plate round again. The midday and evening meals both included meat and vegetables and again one could go round as many times as needed.

We regularly received warnings from the doctors that over-eating could be very dangerous, although in fact after the first day or two of second helpings, very few men wanted more than the one good ration. I weighed slightly less than 6 stones (37 kilo or 82 lb) when I went into that camp and almost 9 stones when I came out!

One of the first things I did was to send a telegram home to my parents; prior to then there having been no opportunity at all. After about two weeks in the camp I went to a barber and enjoyed a nearly normal haircut. My hair was still fairly short on top but it could be combed and parted, more or less into my pre-war style; and all that good head of hair had grown in about ten weeks.

After our evening meal there was a film show when, in addition to the newsreel, there was a reading of the news over the amplifier. On one occasion we heard of uprisings in what was then the Dutch East Indies, but now known as Indonesia. Apparently the natives were rising against the Dutch and I regret to say that the news brought an immediate roar of derisive laughter. Our camp in Mizumaki-cho had been dominated by the Dutch and, to judge from that roar of delighted laughter, so had many others.

I recall another interesting incident. One night I had been to the cinema and having returned to my tent I saw that while my end was empty, there were eight or ten men sitting on the cots at the other end. I did not recognise any of them and, after a quick look at the kit under the bed, I realised that I was in the wrong tent; the correct number but the wrong street. I sat for a moment because my legs ached, and while I did so it became obvious that the subject under heated discussion was the British Royal Family. Further eavesdropping revealed that some four or five Americans were deriding the idea of a monarchy, while about the same number of Australians were defending it. Two points quickly became very clear to me: first that the Americans, in spite of all their arguments, would have given a lot to have their own Royal Family. Secondly I realised that those four or five 'diggers' knew more about the British Royal Family than I or any other average Englishman would. Not wishing to be called a 'pom' or a 'goddam limey', or both, I crept away and back to my proper tent.

On one occasion, only a few days before leaving the Manila Transit Camp, we were asked to assemble in a large open area where we were to be addressed by Lady Mountbatten. I attended, as did quite a large number, but I was very disappointed. The Lady Edwina spoke well enough but I found her to be almost unsufferably patronising. As we moved away, all rather disgusted, I espied RSM Peter Scullion of the 155 but, as we could never in any sense have been called friends, I avoided contact. I was then stopped by Captain McKenzie, also of the 155, who told me that we should soon be leaving by troopship to San Francisco, when he would be Officer Commanding Troops. I thanked him for the news, we exchanged information about health and past wanderings, and promised to meet again, but we never did.

On 17th October 1945 we left the transit camp in Manila and embarked on a troopship: the USS Marine Shark, delighted to hear that on its maiden voyage to Manila it had made record speed. We set out on the 7,500-mile journey across the Pacific to San Francisco, making excellent time and full of hope and excitement. Stories had reached us to the effect that previous shiploads of returning FEPOWs (Far East Prisoners of War) had been entertained by the Town of San Francisco for a week, followed by several days in New York, where the Red Cross had taken them sightseeing and to the theatre.

Several days were spent just lounging on deck in the hot sunshine. From our arrival in the transit camp in Manila until we arrived in New York, we received a daily free issue of tobacco: forty cigarettes, four cigars and half an ounce of pipe tobacco. I gathered that it came straight from the tobacco companies who, clearly, wanted to be sure that we were 'hooked' again after so long in enforced abstinence. I was never dominated by the need to smoke and so when, in the camp, cigarettes were scarce, and so was food, I preferred to use my very small supply of 'fags' to buy extra food. On the other hand, some of the men were so desperate for a smoke that they swapped food, including what little protein we received, for cigarettes - and soon paid the ultimate penalty. Needless to say, no one could consume all that daily issue, even though on the Marine Shark we had nothing else to do but smoke all day. I consumed about twenty cigarettes a day, and enjoyed a cigar in the cool of the evening, but the rest went into my 'big pack' and were brought home.

Sleeping on the Marine Shark was in triple-tiered bunks like those on the USS Wadsworth, and the air conditioning on all lower decks was excellent. Meals were served in a large canteen, complete with the inevitable pressed steel trays. On the mess tables, in addition to the milk and sugar, salt and pepper, were bowls of large white tablets which we were told was salt, to be taken, we were advised, with every meal to compensate for that lost in perspiration in the hot climate. I had trouble with those salt tablets! No matter whether I swallowed the tablet before, during or after the meal, in all cases after about a minute I had to dash away to vomit. I abandoned the idea after three days of trying.

Another medication, which we all received more or less continuously from leaving Nagasaki until we landed in San Francisco, was mepacrine tablets (called atabrine by the Americans). These were as a defence and cure for malaria but as there was no incidence of that disease in any of the places on our homeward journey and as, mercifully, I had never had it, there did not seem to be much point. However, it was prescribed and issued, so I took it. The effects did not show immediately but soon we all assumed a distinctly yellow hue under our boot-brown sunburn. Having returned home, the yellow colouring lingered like the effects of jaundice long after the sun tan had faded.

After about five days of speeding across the ocean our new troopship developed troubles in the main bearing of the propeller shaft, and we slowed to a crawl, eventually limping into Pearl Harbour in the failing light of evening. Waiting on the quayside was a white-suited brass band, complete with four sousaphones. Also waiting was a gang of engineer fitters with a replacement bearing.

Apparently members of the crew were permitted to go ashore but the FEPOWS were not. I was interested in the process of changing the bearing so I asked permission from an engineer officer and was allowed to stand on a gallery above the offending bearing. I spent most of the night there, fascinated by the process and the very business-like approach. My friend brought me a cup of tea in the small hours and stayed to chat for a while.

Soon after dawn we were ready to sail again and once more set off at a good speed for the 2,300-mile voyage to San Francisco. Unfortunately, however, we were soon in trouble again. According to the story that went round the ship, the port watch went ashore for the evening and when they returned to duty they fired up the boiler but forgot to put in the water! So went the tale, and I don't know how true it was. Anyway, the result was that once again we were hove to in mid-Pacific while strange thumps and groans came from the bowels of the ship. We wallowed like that, engineless and just turning about with the breeze, for most of one day while the noises continued. I spent as much time as possible up on deck, enjoying the sunshine, but on one occasion that day I became very thirsty and went down to my sleeping quarters where there were several ice-water dispensers. I was amused to see a large number of British FEPOWS sitting all over that deck, mostly on the lowest bunks, busily playing 'Housey Housey'. My amusement was because every one of those men, I should guess at least a hundred, without any orders to do so, were wearing their 'Mae West' life jackets.

Eventually, we were moving again, but at a very slow pace, and that delay was to rob us of our anticipated entertainment in San Francisco and in New York. We arrived off the Golden Gate, the entrance to San Francisco Harbour, a little after dawn on a clear bright day, 3rd November 1945. I can still see mentally the view as we approached. The famous suspension bridge and the flanking hills were still in black silhouette against the early dawn sky, and I was delighted to see that it was indeed golden coloured. Still one or two miles out to sea, there was no sign of any welcome except for that beautiful dawn, but as the daylight increased we could see huge white letters just below the skyline. As their message became readable I could hear dozens of murmured voices around me, all saying the words that they had wanted to hear for so very long a time: WELCOME HOME.

Soon most of the ship's company had finished their toilet and a hasty breakfast and were 'topside'. There was little tangible display of emotion but one could sense a growing feeling of excitement, particularly among the Americans. The next thing to attract my attention was the suspension bridge, seen by most of us for the first time. As we approached I felt sure that our tall masts would not pass under it but the general perspective and the dawn light were playing strange tricks with one's ability, even as an old gunner, to judge distance and size. When we did sail beneath it the bridge deck was so high above us that our quite large troopship felt like a little fishing smack.

Just inside the bay, the first vessel to approach us was a ferry boat which, after several long hoots on its whistle, turned and kept pace with us. A middle-aged man with a loud hailer greeted us and read a brief speech of welcome, after which a Women's Army band struck up and played several tunes. I couldn't hear them, though. Soon we were joined by seemingly dozens of other small craft, all tooting their whistles and horns. A fire tender arrived, soon to be joined by several others, and the plume-shaped fountains from their hoses glinted like diamante ornaments in the early morning sunshine.

The spokesman on the ferryboat then called across: 'Marine Shark! Do you have Lieutenant Jack Jones on board? We have a message from his wife,' The band played another tune and then again came the call: 'Marine Shark! Is Lieutenant Jones there?' 'Yeah, he's here.' was shouted back. Whereupon, a plump little lady in the band put down her saxophone, came across to the microphone and shouted: 'Hello, Jack!' The whole ship seemed to erupt! The entire company either shouted 'Hello' or gave a wolf whistle, and the Captain or someone on the bridge joined in by tooting the ship's siren.

As we steamed steadily into the harbour more and more ships and small boats joined us and the noise increased. There was a rather peculiar and moving moment when we sailed past a rocky islet, and above the general din we heard vociferous cheering coming from buildings on top of its rugged cliffs. Looking more closely, we could see the faces and hands of the prisoners of Alcatraz as they gripped the bars of their windows and peered out, shouting at the tops of their voices.

When the time came for us to approach our berth, instructions for leaving the ship came over the loudspeakers on all decks, and I recognised Captain

McKenzie's voice. The Americans were to go ashore first, followed by the British, deck by deck. Would we all please go below, collect all our gear and wait until called. None of us wanted to leave the upper decks because there was still plenty happening, but we were an orderly rabble and in any case we had been asked most politely. We all went quietly to our decks and waited.

Quite a long time later, it was my turn to move out. My route led along a very narrow passageway and I got stuck in it. On my back was my original 'big pack' and balanced on it and my bent shoulders was the recently issued large kit bag. Neither was very heavy, being filled largely with cigarettes and other 'comforts' that had been so generously given to us, but I was very weak and found little spare strength when the kitbag became wedged across the narrow passage. This delayed me for a while, and the same thing happened to the man behind me so that I came down the gangway quite alone. Bent over beneath my burden, legs wobbling as I stumbled down the slope and with my battered and much-repaired spectacles almost slipping off my nose, I was surprised to hear clapping. Peering up as best I could, I had a blurred sight of the quayside and two rows of deck chairs, with the mayor and all the dignitaries of the town sitting there to greet us. I felt a real fool, the more so because I could do nothing to acknowledge this courteous greeting given so generously to a foreigner.

Seeing on television in 1982 the faces of the Gurkha soldiers as they stood at the rails of the SS Uganda when she returned from the Falkland Islands to Plymouth after her duty as a hospital ship, my wife remarked that they must feel very sad and bemused when they were still very far from their own home. Perhaps they did. I don't know, but I doubt that because I certainly felt very much a part of the occasion when we were welcomed by the good and generous people of San Francisco. As I write this note it is difficult to realise that that occasion was so very long ago. It seems like only yesterday.

I stumbled on past the Welcoming Party and soon found myself with my comrades being marshalled into some sense of order by a WAC Sergeant with a voice in the upper registers. She took a lot of kindly banter but eventually got us to move as a continuous single file across the quay to a ferry boat similar to the one which had come out to meet the ship at the Golden Gate. When I boarded the ferry I was met by a WAC Top Sergeant who, my luck, then decided that the lower deck was full.

With a crisp 'Come this way, Sonny!' she led me along the deck and then went up a broad stair to the upper deck. I started to climb but just had not the strength and could get no further than the first step. That Top Sergeant was tall, willowy, very good looking, and to my ex-POW eyes almost unbelievable. She looked down from the top step and, seeing my difficulty, came back down again. 'What's the matter, Sonny? Can't you make it?' and without waiting for my halting reply, she picked up my kit bag under her left arm, picked me up, big pack and all with her right arm and carried me up the stairs. Then she walked along the upper deck, set down the kit bag on its end, turned and sat me on top of it. She reached into her breast pocket for a packet of cigarettes, flipped one out, stuck it in my mouth, produced a lighter and lit the cigarette, patting me on the head saying: 'There you are! Sit there, Sonny 'til we get to Fort McDowell!' I guess she was about twenty-two years old. I was twenty-six and felt like eighty-six.

Fort McDowell, a smallish island in San Francisco Bay, was being used as a de-briefing and kitting out station for returning British troops. We spent an afternoon and a night there and received a new Canadian Army battle dress, complete with shirts, tie, underclothes, boots and a greatcoat. Those were the first decent clothes I had seen, let alone worn, since being taken prisoner in Singapore three and a half years earlier. My companions and I had a good hot shower and then dressed ourselves with some excitement.

In the dressing room were several full-length mirrors, the significance of which merits some explanation. We had not had mirrors for a long time but had grown accustomed to seeing each other as scraggy and emaciated wretches, and I still thought of myself as being like that. Then, wearing only my new battle dress trousers, I caught sight of a figure to my side and at first glance did not recognise that the heavily sun-tanned and well-padded, muscular looking man was really the scraggy weedy youth I had thought was me. I stopped in my tracks and postured and preened in front of the mirror, but then, realising what I was doing, hurriedly moved on, glancing round quickly to see if anyone had noticed my vanity. Not at all. They were all doing it!

Then came the shirt, which fitted very well, and the necktie which most of us had forgotten how to tie. Some practiced by tying it round the thigh, and there was a lot of muttering and helping of each other. Once the ties were on, all the preening started again. We were as proud as peacocks. The fact that our so-called muscles, which we could flex and ripple, were only 'water fat', the result of some over-feeding after years of very hard work on a starvation diet, was forgotten. What did it matter? We were going home to our families looking good.

We were given a light meal and then went for what was called de-briefing. I cannot remember exactly what we had to do, but it involved form-filling and answering a lot of questions about our POW days, and it took all night. We got no sleep at all. We were issued with new British Army pay books and given a small sum of United States dollars. 'Can't have any more. There's a dollar crisis, you know.' We didn't know, and were very disappointed because all hoped to be able to buy some presents for our families. I think our total issue of cash was twenty dollars; not sufficient even for our quite modest needs.

Next morning, after a breakfast that we were almost too sleepy to eat, we were ferried across to Oakland and to a hospital train wherein we all travelled head first and horizontal in bed. While being most grateful for the thought and consideration behind this, I was disappointed because I wanted to see the scenery, and that was very difficult when it was moving rapidly from top to bottom across one's vision. I was in an upper berth and although there was room to sit up in bed, the window was then far too low to see out. I tried to explain to the attending doctor, a US Army Captain, that I was simply very weak and not really ill, but he could do nothing because the whole train was fitted with bunk beds. The result was that my impression of the State of Oregon was rather peculiar, the rail-side on the left being flanked by horizontal pine trees and the occasional vertical stretch of water!

Our train journey took us about eight hundred miles north to Tacoma, famous, we learned, as the birth place of Bing Crosby, and it took about twenty hours so that we spent the night of Friday, 2nd November in bed on the train. During the journey we received frequent bedside visits, not only from the doctor but also from uniformed ladies of the Red Cross and also, I think, other similar organisations. From them we received another cloth drawstring bag of comforts similar to that given in Nagasaki, and an assortment of chocolate bars and other sweets. Also, although we did not really need it, there was a continuing supply of tobacco, cigarettes and cigars. I don't remember what food we had on the train; only that it was difficult to eat while in one's bunk. In the afternoon of Sunday, 4th November the train stopped in Tacoma, a seaport on Puget Sound in the State of Washington. From the train, which appeared to have stopped at nowhere in particular in the middle of the town, buses took us about fifteen miles inland to an army camp where we spent four nights.

The atmosphere in that camp was similar to that in all the other camps we had visited since leaving Japan. Cheerful and slightly unreal, or 'phoney' would be fair. The 'in' tune at that time was: 'Drinking Rum and Coca Co-la' and one heard it played almost everywhere. There was an abundance of food of excellent quality but, in spite of big notices posted around the mess halls, much of it was wasted by being left on the plates. It hurt me to see, remembering that I had seen men fight - no! that's not right! I had fought - for less than was nonchalantly left to be scooped into the waste bin. Some of us protested but it was useless. Nobody cared. Fingers were snapped, hips were wiggled - and all to the tune of 'Rum and Coca Co-la'.

On three successive mornings we were able to take a bus back into Tacoma to do some shopping for presents to take home to our families. At first, and as soon as our battledress uniforms were seen, many of the shops closed their doors firmly and put up their shutters; the reason, I was told, being that only a week or so earlier a similar invasion had occurred and the town had been taken apart. However, as soon as it was understood that we were returning British FEPOWs and not Canadians, the shops all opened again. Also, people would stop us in the street, just to talk. One young matron, aged perhaps thirty five or so, stopped me to ask: 'Say! Are you English?' When I said that I was, she continued: 'Gee! Do you know Mrs Gwynne Jones? She lives in Cardiff.' I tried to explain but I'm sure the lady didn't understand, and probably never would.

When our fellows went shopping they were looking almost exclusively for gifts for their women folk, but then there was a problem because none had any idea of size or fit for anything. The first recourse was to rush around the store until they found one of the shop assistants who appeared to be about the right size. Then that young lady, willy-nilly, had to model the chosen garment. That first day was quite hilarious and as one walked down the street the sounds of laughter, mostly female, could be heard coming from all the clothes shops. Incidentally, I solved my own problem by buying handbags, but even then it wasn't easy because the American idea of a neat handbag would have served to carry one's tennis racquets. And they called them purses!

On the second day the town was much better organised. Word must have travelled round the town to the effect that if properly handled we were quite harmless, and so, as soon as our buses arrived and the men went into the shops they would be greeted by the manager and a 'chorus line' of every female assistant in the shop, irrespective of age. All the men had to do was to walk down the line until they saw a woman who, according to their memory of about five years ago, was the right size. Some of the shops even offered cups of 'cor-fee'. Great fun!

Early on Thursday, 8th November, we were collected by a small fleet of buses and were set down in the middle of the town to wait in the cold half-light. Eventually a train arrived, backing slowly in from the north, and I wondered how, without a platform, one could climb up into the coach that towered above me. Then the doors were opened and negro attendants let down steps. We climbed aboard and discovered that it was a Canadian National Railway train, which was to take us on a five days and five nights journey across Canada and thence to New York. The reason for travelling across Canada rather than by the more direct route from San Francisco across the States was because of the already met shortage of US dollars.

The train was devoted entirely to returning British POWs, of which I seemed to be the only one from the 155, although many years later I discovered that a large number had been in the forward part of the train. The coaches were filled to only half their normal capacity so that each FEPOW had a double seat. At night a high-level bunk over the facing pair of seats was lowered by the attendant, and one of us slept in it while the other had a bed made by extending the daytime seating. All very comfortable, and the food was excellent, although getting from one's seat to the dining car was always a difficult exercise. I was told that whereas the rail joints in Britain are opposite, those in the USA and Canada are staggered. The result, for whatever reason, was that the coaches swung from side to side so that walking along the train corridor was exceedingly difficult. Then it needed a lot of practice to take soup, to pour tea, and even to drink from a cup or glass.

Our route took us over the Rockies via Jasper National Park, with Mount Rainier just visible in the mist; and I have vivid memories of the rugged scenery that, in wintertime, was all black and white. I bought some picture postcards somewhere along the way and their black and white photos looked just like the original scenes.

The weather was exceedingly cold as we crossed the Rockies, with temperatures of about minus 15 degrees Fahrenheit, or 47 degrees of frost (equal to minus 26 degrees Celsius) at midday. The train stopped once or twice to fill up with coal and water and we were permitted to get out and stretch our legs for fifteen minutes, warned not to go out without our greatcoats and to keep the collar turned up to protect the ears from frost bite. On one occasion, suitably covered up, I noticed a strange feeling in my nostrils as they filled with small icicles, and when I spat on the ground, just to see what would happen, it landed with a 'clonk', frozen solid before it landed. At one stop I walked along to have a look at the engine and was greatly impressed by its size. The driving wheels appeared to be at least twice my height.

The train also stopped briefly at one or two big towns, when it was invaded by young women whose main aim in life seemed to be to invite us to 'Hev some more cor-fee!' At the same time papers were handed out which exhorted us to join the Canadian army, the arrangement being that as soon as the paper was signed and handed in, the man would be enlisted but would be on several months of leave. During that time the new recruit would receive pay by post. I thought it was an irresponsible idea, not only to offer the recruitment but also to accept it when having no idea of affairs at home. However, a few men did sign, but I think they were bewitched by those lovely young ladies with their seductive voices urging us to have 'some more cor-fee!'

Our last stop on the way was in Toronto, after which we went across the border, back into The States and on to New York where, alas, there was no time to stop and see the town. We went directly aboard the Queen Mary in the failing light of Thursday, 13th November, and we sailed next morning. My only real recollection of that very brief stop in New York was of looking over the rail at the murky waters of the dock, which appeared to be liberally strewn with 'french-letters' (condoms) scattered at about one per square yard.

The five days sail across the Atlantic was uneventful; almost boring. The cold and damp November weather deterred us from spending much time on deck and there was little to occupy us between meals. Most of us just strolled quietly around the 'indoor' parts of the ship, but even the topic of 'what I'm going to do when I get home' was wearing thin. We were very disappointed, almost horrified, to discover that we were back to the old 'swill bucket' method of feeding which, after our experiences on American ships, was not appreciated and was the subject of many adverse comments.

We heard that there were some civilian passengers and that one of them, said to be Alexander Korda, had complained to the captain about troops invading his 'private area', but the story went on to report that the captain had replied that after these men's experiences, so long as they left the funnels in place they were welcome to the whole ship. Really, there were very few troops on board, most of them returning FEPOWs, and although there were no recognisable units, no chain of command and, apart from doctors, no officers in sight since we left San Francisco, yet we were a very quiet and orderly lot. I even heard plenty of disapproving comment about the graffiti on the walls, and in particular about the almost total carving of the wooden rails round the decks. There were names, numbers and places of origin by the thousands, and the greater part of them were Australian.

During our approach to the English Channel before dawn on the 19th November (my mother's birthday) there were some signs of emotion. Even in the darkness the rails were crowded as men peered ahead into the mist, hoping to see the Isles of Scilly, the Bishop Rock light or any sign of 'home'. In fact, because of the mist, almost nothing was visible until we sailed into Southampton in the late morning. There was no sign of a reception, not even a friendly toot from a nearby vessel, until we were alongside our berth when a man standing on the quay recognised his son who, presumably, was leaning over the rail like the rest of us. That father let out such a shout that it echoed round the whole neighbourhood, not only reaching his long lost son but also leaving quite a bit over for the rest of us. With no other welcoming parties at that time, we all were delighted to share what was going and soon an echoing cheer went around the ship.

After about twenty minutes a band marched onto the quay and began to play but there was another long delay before we went ashore, each carrying all his possessions. By that time it was about 1.30 p.m. and we were shepherded into a large shed wherein were long rows of trestle tables covered with white cloths and all set for a meal. As we filed slowly into the shed a sergeant standing by the door observed that there was 'a special meal for you lads. Pity you're so late. It's been ready since noon' By then it was after 2 p.m.! The meal was roast beef and Yorkshire pudding, and I forget what was for 'afters'. We could well understand that to a war-weary and half-starved Britain it really was a special meal but, after at least two hours of waiting, the meat was hard and dry, the Yorkshire pudding was like rubber, and the pint of beer sitting at every place was completely flat. Ah, well! While in the shed we were each handed a large brown envelope containing a printed message of welcome and thanks from the King.

After the meal we were shown to billets where we were to spend one night and we were told that after 6 p.m. there would be a free telephone service for us to call our folks. Rail warrants were made out and I had only a little trouble in persuading the sergeant to make mine via Liverpool instead of Chester. When I made my telephone call I was able to wish my mother a very happy birthday, which she assured me it was. Then my father commented: 'Well, lad, you've been right round! But tell me, were you walking it?' Both Mum and Dad were at Liverpool Lime Street station to meet me at about 6 p.m. on 20th November, 1945.

My father had been a pilot on the Manchester Ship Canal since the end of The Great War, during which he served in the 'Wavy Navy' as Lieutenant and Navigating Officer, and he was on the flagship at the Battle of Jutland. There were several other pilots and master mariners living near us, each of whom had their own flagstaffs in their gardens, and there was a very large amount of bunting on display as we drove up to our home.

The army kept me on 'hold' for another three months, during which time I received pay and also coupons for food and sweets, etc. My mind was just a little stiff and I foresaw problems with the studying of the structural engineering I had decided was to be my new career. Then a neighbour and friend, Bill Lyon, then recently retired from the Headship of Birkenhead School of Commerce, offered to give me some maths lessons, saying he could think of nothing better to sharpen the brain. It worked, and by Christmas I felt ready to tackle the work ahead.

The Government was reputed to be willing to send returning servicemen to university if a reasonable case could be made, and I heard from Jim Warner, met in the camp in Japan, that he was to begin reading medicine. Thus encouraged, I applied to be sent to Liverpool to read Civil Engineering and was amazed when a 'grateful government' replied that I could go back to reading Architecture but there would be no sponsorship to start afresh on Civil Engineering. I was disappointed and very annoyed but was in no mood to be 'messed about' by any civil servants. I extended two fingers in the direction of London, made arrangements to begin studies at the Tech in evening classes, and on 2nd January 1945, I went back to John Clarke and Son, with whom I had been for a few months before being called up in 1939. I got my professional qualifications four years later, the hard way.

I was discharged down in Devizes on 15th March 1946 and sent back into 'civvy street' complete with a good quality new suit and a new paybook which, apart from my number, rank and name, contained only the note of discharge. The reason given for said discharge was an item in the Army Act which, when translated, amounted to me being: 'Not amenable to good order and military discipline'. I suppose that was correct, bearing in mind that any British prison would be like a rest camp compared with where we had been for so long. However, as already observed, we were in fact a very biddable rabble, particularly when the word 'please' was added to any request.

CHAPTER TEN

TO JAPAN TO LAY A GHOST

Back home, my one thought was to rebuild the career that had been interrupted in 1939, but this time as a structural engineer rather than as an architect. I worked hard and long at my new calling and there was no room in my thoughts for memories of the war, even though there was an intense hatred in my heart. I tell you frankly that had I been introduced to a Japanese in your house I should have spat on your carpet and walked out. However, night time was different and for several years after the war I had nightmares, perhaps two or three times a week, when I would be chased down dark mine passages by a hoard of Nips, all looking like The Pig. Then, as time passed, the nightmares stopped, to be replaced by wakeful nights when I would argue with The Pig in an attempt to show that I was not the ignorant coolie that, apparently, he took me to be. You know how it goes. After an important meeting or interview one lives through it all over again, saying in one's imagination all the fine things one should have said - if only one could have thought of them at the time! And, because I knew that Maeda, The Pig, had no English, all that argument had to be in the very poor Japanese that I had secretly learned in the camp.

This sort of thing went on for a long time, for nearly twenty years in fact, and it was not until 1965 that I had a change of thought. All that hating was doing me a lot of harm and no good at all. It had to be stopped.

The only way I could think of to lay the ghost of The Pig and all he represented was to go back to Japan, to find that one man, and to make friends with him. Some of my family and friends thought I was quite mad but would have understood if I had wanted to give Maeda a good beating. However, I knew that would only have revived the hate. Unfortunately, at that time Japan was expensively beyond my reach, so I bought a pocket dictionary and a book of Japanese grammar and prepared to wait. In 1968 our daughter left school, leaving me better off by several pounds a week of taxed income. Then, in October of the same year, my Chief retired and I got the Chief's job. By next year the trip to Japan had become a possibility. One day in 1969 when I was in London on business, I called at the Japanese Embassy where I told the gist of the story and asked if they could find Maeda. At first they were rather suspicious, thinking that I was on a punitive raid, but eventually, and happily, they became convinced of my sincerity and quickly set about finding Maeda. Incidentally, they explained that Maeda is a very common name in Japan; about as common as Smith is here. They wrote to their foreign office in Tokyo, who wrote to the Home Office, who wrote to the North Kyushu Miners' Association.

Apparently there had been two men called Maeda in charge of prisoners in the Fukuoka district. One, deceased, would have been about 80 years of age while the other, called Chuzo Maeda, was 57. I was then 49 and I knew that The Pig had been a few years older than me, but that was not enough. I had no intention of travelling 7,000 miles there and 7,000 miles back, only to find that we had the wrong man, so I asked another question: Had the 57-year old Maeda been *nana buntai cho*? About a fortnight later, back from the Japanese Embassy came a letter out of which fell two photographs. One taken in 1945, was unmistakably the Pig while the other was of a kindly looking middle-aged Japanese gentleman - with the same pimple on his nose. We'd found him!

I wrote a letter in very inexpert Japanese to Maeda-san (san is the courtesy title: Mr, Mrs, or Miss), asking if he would be willing to meet me, and he replied that he would be proud to do so. A small reception would be arranged in my honour, with about seventy people being present. Gosh! And all I wanted was a quiet meeting with Maeda-san. Ah, well! I arranged for my wife and me to join a party going to Japan in March, 1970, on what was euphemistically called an Architectural Study Tour and to visit Expo-70 at Osaka, and then a meeting with

Maeda-san was arranged for Sunday, 22nd March. When that day dawned, my wife Dea and I left our party in Osaka and flew some three hundred miles to Fukuoka where, Maeda had said, we should be met. As we walked up the long exit passage I was a head taller than most of the crowd and looking anxiously ahead for some sign of recognition. We were a long way from home, in a foreign land and only partially understanding the language, but we needn't have worried. Half-way up the gangway on the left hand side was a special exit where stood a young man holding up a large piece of paper on which was written: WELCOME TO MR. RODESU AND MRS. RODESS. This could only have been for us and we turned to meet a small party. Immediately, a pretty young lady in a very colourful kimono stepped forward and in quite good English said that she was Toshiko Maeda, she was to welcome us to Kyushu and to take us to her uncle. Then she pinned huge white rosettes on us and invited us to get into a waiting car. Well, you should have seen that car! Large and shiny black, it was covered all over with tinsel of red, gold, shocking pink and silver. Across the front of the bonnet were a Union Flag and a *Hi no Maru* (Sun's circle), the Japanese flag. Fixed to the left-hand front was a long black and yellow pole to which was attached a much larger Union Flag; upside down as was the smaller one on the bonnet. Dea remarked that they were our distress signals.

With Dea and me in the back, Toshiko sat in front between the driver and a man in dark blue uniform, later identified as the Chief of the local Fire Brigade of which, apparently, Maeda-san was the Honorary Chairman. We set off on the 45-mile drive from Fukuoka Airport eastward to Mizumaki-cho, the village location of the coal mine and the old prison camp. The driver went as quickly as he could on the narrow and often poorly surfaced roads, sounding the horn to attract attention and often on the wrong side of the road (they drive on the left like the British). Oncoming traffic, pedestrians and chickens just had to get out of the way as best they could. The local people must have learned from the morning papers of our coming because for much of the way the road was lined with Japanese, all waving Union Flags and bowing low. Dea and I waved back happily, pretending that we were Elizabeth and Philip!

Arrived at Mizumaki-cho, the driver sounded the horn for quite a long time to warn of our coming and then drove up to the front of the village hall. There I saw Maeda-san standing, surrounded by a large number of men, all wearing gold chains. Apparently, every lord mayor and mayor from miles around had turned up for the occasion. Inside the hall we were ushered through a huge crowd, all shouting: 'Aro, Rozu-san!', to below a small stage where two young girls in pretty kimono stepped forward and gave Dea a big sheaf of flowers. That was fine, but then two more came forward and gave me a similar bunch. I felt very awkward but managed quickly to dispose of it onto a nearby windowsill.

Then a gentleman named Takahashi (no relation of the erstwhile sergeant) stepped forward and gave a long speech of explanation and welcome, after which he read out a sheaf of greetings telegrams. There was one from the local MP, one from the Governor of Fukuoka-ken, and one from a man who signed himself simply as 'statesman', as well as many from old miners and fire brigade friends of Maeda. Next, Takahashi introduced a succession of men who came forward to give me presents. The first gift was a much be-ribboned parcel which, when opened, revealed a beautiful vase of green enamel on cast copper. Inscribed in gold on the base, in Japanese characters, was the message: 'To Peter S. Rhodes-san. A gift from Hikaro Kamei, Governor of Fukuoka-ken.' Then three men, old miners I think, stepped forward. Two carried parcels while the third had an airline poster that he proceeded to unroll. Then the three in unison explained that the one parcel contained a Hakata Doll (Hakata is the old name for Fukuoka), the second contained the glass case and, please, I needn't open either because they looked just like the poster.

A man whom I thought I had seen before then came forward and gave me a beautiful silk tie. His card, read for me later by a friend, proclaimed that he was Kyuichi Yamazaki, president of the local Red Cross, of several motoring organisations and also of the funeral company which had supplied the decorated car. He was in fact our crazy driver! He was followed by an elderly man: Isamu Maeda (no relation) carrying a large piece of white paper on which he had written, in Chinese characters: 'For this beautiful meeting of friendship-congratulations.' Attached to the paper was an old and beautiful print which now, framed, hangs in my home. Finally Maeda-san came up to give me his own personal gift, another silk tie. I immediately removed my Structural Engineers tie and, amid applause, donned Maeda's gift.

Takahashi then said that that concluded the formal business and we would now eat, but I took the microphone to say: Oh, no. It was now my turn. I gave an eighteen-minute speech in tolerably good Japanese, correcting some small errors in Takahashi's introduction and then going on to tell something of POW days. In doing so I was able to make one or two jokes which brought roars of laughter. Then I gave Maeda-san my gift to him. As presented it looked like a small box, a little larger than a matchbox, tied up in a square of purple rayon. It was in fact a model of my *bento baku* or picnic lunch box in which I had carried my meagre ration of plain boiled rice. Inside were small models of a woven bamboo basket, called an *ebu*, and a short-handled scraper called a *kake-ita*. They were made by myself out of beaten copper which was then silver plated. In giving them to Maeda-san I said, in Japanese: 'During the war we were enemies. Now, happily, we are friends and in token of this I give you back my miners' tools.' Maeda recognised them immediately and held them up delightedly for all to see, while the cine and TV cameras zoomed in. Then I gave him some Irish Linen handkerchiefs bearing his *roma ji* (Roman letters) initial 'M', and to Mrs. Maeda an Irish Linen Damask tablecloth.

Well, that really did conclude the formalities, and food and drink were served, but I was so busy being introduced to old miners and having my photo taken that my lunch consisted of three glasses of champagne and three untouched plates of food. There seemed to be dozens of firemen, all in full dress uniform. It was just as well there wasn't a fire that day! Some youngsters sang some songs and Mr. Isamu Maeda demonstrated some old dances and some ancient samurai weapons and fighting techniques.

Then it was time to move on, first to the old mine head, long closed, and then on to Maeda's home. On the way out of the hall, a slow process, everyone wanted to shake hands and I estimated that the number present was about 150, rather more than the 70 originally mentioned, and the noise and applause was deafening.

The first visit was to the mine head where 'bentonite', a variety of drilling mud, was being processed, and then to the old camp which, to my surprise, was still there, although it had lost the tall boundary fence. Somebody knocked at a house door in what had been the old hospital block, and when it was opened I could see the surprised occupants sitting on the floor and playing cards, just like we had done. Memories of the past came flooding back, but these were soon dispelled by the sight of happy children playing where, once, half-starved prisoners had skulked.

Next, at Maeda's home I thought I might have a chance for a quiet talk with him, but no. Soon the house was full of firemen and old miners, and more food was served. Eventually the party broke up and it was time to go back to the airport. Maeda came with us and then, for about an hour, we had some chance to talk.

Arrived at the plane, we climbed aboard with all our flowers and beribboned parcels. Some of the passenger knew who we were and smiled Others just recognised that we were foreigners who had been give 'the treatment'! But one lady, an American, came up to us and said: 'We do like your luggage!' It all arrived home safely and now there are many souvenirs to remind me of a most happy and successful visit. As I said at the time: the ghost of The Pig and the war was well and truly laid.

I gathered later that the meeting with Maeda-san had been reported in virtually all publications in Japan, as well as by all Radio and TV channels. It was also reported in Australia and the West Coast of the USA, but there was little mention of it in this country because I needed to keep a quiet name. However, soon after returning home, I began to receive letters which fell into three categories and with quite a lot in each. The first group were from mothers and wives or widows of ex-Far East Prisoners Of War. Without exception they disapproved of my visit, and some sent their curses. They were very unpleasant letters and I burned the lot.

The second group were from ex-FEPOWs. I didn't really know any of them but they had -my name and address from somewhere. Without exception, they approved, applauded, and envied. The third group were from sixteen-year old Japanese boys and girls who had got my address from an agency, and they all wanted to be pen-pals. Well, here was a chance to spread a little friendship and understanding instead of hate, so I took on the lot, becoming Uncle Peter or Peter Ojisan to what seemed like half of the youth of Japan.

I went back alone to Japan for a month in 1973 with the intention of meeting the people and walking as a free man up all the little back streets which once were barred to me. I met most of my new 'nephews' and 'nieces' and found quite a few more. Now, of course, most of those youngsters are married and with families of their own, so I am now 'Great Uncle Peter'. I was back again for a month-long visit in 1980, about a month after Maeda-san had died of diabetes.

Then in 1984 NHK (Nihon Hoso Kaisha, the Japan Broadcasting Corporation) had me back to Mizumaki-cho to make a thirty-minute video which they called, in translation, 'The Blue Eyed Miner - Peter Rhodes'. In it I told of many of the bad things which had been done, and the video was shown on NHK TV in the Kyushu area, when it evoked several written responses from the viewing audience. Incidentally, the Japanese referred to all the European prisoners as *Aoi me*, or 'Blue eyes', theirs being generally dark brown or black.

A typical response, from a young woman schoolteacher, said that she was horrified to learn of what had been done. She had never known anything about such things and thought that the video should be screened at least once a year as a reminder of what had been done by her parents' generation, and as a reminder not to do it again.

Many people have asked if I heard the Atom Bomb at Nagasaki, and I may have done so but there were so many bangs and so much noise from the compressors at the mine that I would not have noticed it. And what did we think of it at the time? Well, nothing really, until, as already described, we were on our way home. But then I have been asked many times and particularly by Japanese people, what I thought of it in retrospect. Then I have described the incident of the U-shaped tunnel and have concluded that, in the event of an invasion, the whole Japanese nation was so indoctrinated that they would have fought to the death - of the lot of us. The atom bombs stopped that invasion, so you may understand that I and most of my fellow POWs in Japan were very grateful for them. Even now, after so many years, I am sure it was the right thing to do.

More recently I was asked what I thought about the Duke of Edinburgh going to the funeral of the late Emperor Hirohito, and my answer has always been short and simple. I disapproved most strongly. The reason is that whatever we suffered in brutality, cuts in food, or the preparation of that U-shaped tunnel, all were proclaimed as being done 'in the name of the Emperor'.

Now I happen to think that he did know what was going on and did indeed authorise the order to 'kill them all and leave no trace'. But even if he did not know or, knowing, personally disapproved, that does not matter. Like it or not, all the crimes committed against us, and the peoples of the invaded countries were done in his name, and his own people accepted that he was omniscient and omnipotent. As an old man I could not find it in my heart to wish death upon another old man, but I drew the line at the Queen's representative, Prince Philip, who probably detested the job, going to pay respects. It sent the wrong signals to more than one generation.

On the other hand, the new Emperor Akihito could not be held to be so responsible. He is of now and of a new era and I should have been glad to go and cheer at his coronation. I have neither forgotten nor forgiven. How could I, bearing in mind what was done? But I have stopped hating and, as the result of much close and personal contact, I find that I like the modern Japanese and am happy to treat them as my friends.

CITRON PRESS